MW00831157

"This book is as clear-eyed a McGinley draws from histor successes. But he applies th are fresh, realistic, and astonishingly creative. There is no other book like this. I hope many readers will take it to heart and take it to prayer."

—Mike Aquilina
Catholic author and speaker

"*The Prodigal Church* is an essential intervention from one of our most exciting young Catholic commentators, offering both a forceful critique of the bourgeois spirit in American Catholicism and a practical, humane road map for renewal."

—Sohrab Ahmari
Op-ed editor, *New York Post*

"McGinley paints the challenging landscape of the modern Church with honesty and clarity. But this book is about more than the challenges we face: it is a brilliant and insightful examination of what the Church can be. No book is more effective at communicating what we must recover, ways to innovate, and how we must act in order to have a thriving Church in the 21st century. McGinley never falls into cynicism or mere wishful thinking but bases his vision on what we can anchor our hope for the future in: the grace of God."

—Haley Stewart
Catholic author, podcaster, and speaker

"Brandon McGinley's book is a bracing work, rooted in a fierce love for the Church and Christ's people. McGinley proposes simply that the Church must be the Church and reminds us how to be rooted and receive what God gives."

—Leah Libresco
Author and blogger

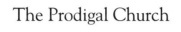

The Prodigal Church

Brandon McGinley

The Prodigal Church
Restoring Catholic Tradition in an Age of Deception

SOPHIA INSTITUTE PRESS
Manchester, New Hampshire

Sophia Institute Press
Box 5284, Manchester, NH 03108
1-800-888-9344

www.SophiaInstitute.com

Sophia Institute Press® is a registered trademark of Sophia Institute.

Library of Congress Cataloging-in-Publication Data

Names: McGinley, Brandon, author.
Title: The prodigal church : restoring Catholic tradition in an age of deception / Brandon McGinley.
Other titles: Renewal two thousand fifty
Description: Manchester, New Hampshire : Sophia Institute Press, 2020. Includes bibliographical references. Summary: "A vision for renewing the Church in America: in the Church itself, the parish, the family, and the community"— Provided by publisher.
Identifiers: LCCN 2020016424 ISBN 9781644132449 ISBN 9781644132456 (ebook)
Subjects: LCSH: Catholic Church—United States—History—21st century. Church renewal—Catholic Church.
Classification: LCC BX1406.3 .M356 2020 DDC 282/.730905—dc23
LC record available at https://lccn.loc.gov/2020016424

First printing

For Katie, who makes everything possible

Contents

Author's Note

When this book reaches your hands, you'll know a lot more about what changed during the COVID-19 outbreak than I did when I wrote it. More importantly, you'll have some idea of which changes were temporary and which calcified into a new normal. It's fruitless for me to speculate about what American life will be like in the second half of 2020 and beyond. Sure, I have some daydreams—some interesting in an exhilarating way, others interesting in a morbid way—but the Lord has not yet blessed me with the gift of prophecy.

You should know that I'm conservative in disposition: I value stability, tradition, permanence. But our secular liberal order offers only the appearance of these social virtues: Its apparent solidity is based in constant motion, obsession with "progress" and "growth" for their own sakes, the perpetual overturning of the past and its replacement with perpetually fading novelty. (How fitting, I suppose, that this order is being tested by a disease caused by a novel virus—a kind of novelty that can't be captured for power or profit.) And so, at least in my less disciplined moments, I welcome a few civilizational tremors, a few shocks that unsettle us from our complacency and comfort. I think something good can come out of crisis, even if we don't desire or certainly enflame any particular crisis that comes our way.

The Prodigal Church

But *this* crisis, this sly pandemic that quietly enlists the strong in its campaign against the weak, seems almost tailor-made to expose the fractures in our political and economic order. It forces an impossible but unavoidable choice between the harms of contagion and the harms of mitigation, between threats to life and threats to order. It attacks the perpetual-motion machine of the economy, on which everything about our material way of life rests, in a way nothing has for generations. And perhaps most insidious of all, it makes us fear the company of our fellow human beings; thus, it is an assault on our very nature and happiness as social beings. Altogether, it makes us wonder if we really did have everything figured out, and it makes us ask ourselves seriously and urgently if there might have been something we missed—about what it means to live in a society and about what it means to be a human being—that left us so vulnerable.

It seems both appropriate and ominous, then, that this crisis has also taken liturgy hostage. I am writing these words, for the first time since my return to the sacraments over a decade ago, without the benefit of recently hearing the Mass and receiving our Lord in Holy Communion. In my diocese, as in most of America and much of the world, public Masses have been suspended. Of course, the Mass itself can never be canceled, not by any earthly power: Priests still celebrate the Sacrifice on their own, and the angels still minister, and the full unity of the Church is still manifested, and grace is still poured out onto the earth. And, of course, we have the opportunity and the duty to make a spiritual communion, uniting ourselves with Christ and His Body, the Church, throughout the world and in purgation and in salvation.

I remind myself of this as a counsel of hope, but it still feels so strange—stranger than the cancellation of March Madness or even the postponement of my beloved Masters. Every day is the same now, if we let it become so. Tuesday gymnastics is canceled.

Author's Note

Thursday playdates are canceled. Friday visits with grandparents are canceled. And Sunday Mass, at least for the laity, is canceled.

But the Sabbath cannot be canceled. And so we dress in "church clothes" and have a little morning liturgy and perform a spiritual communion and make pancakes and try to rest from housework and lawn work and so on. It's a way of consecrating the day, of course, but it's also a way of keeping things normal, of marking the passage of ecclesial time through this Lent, this long Lent.

Nobody knows yet what the world will be like on the other side of this long Lent of pandemic and panic and political upheaval. The wonderful thing, though, about Lent and our Church and our Faith is that we *do* know *Who* is on the other side. Lent always ends with Easter, the Passion with the Resurrection. And the true Faith and the true Church always, even if imperfectly in her earthly institutions, lead us to Christ.

In times of confusion and crisis, people look for the solid things, the permanent things, the sane things. This isn't just what the Church *can be*; it's what the Church *is*. She is solidity in an unstable world, permanence in a temporary world, sanity in a crazy world. This book is a plea—to hierarchs, to priests, and most of all to the faithful—to act like it.

Pittsburgh, Pennsylvania
March 18, 2020

Introduction: A Prophecy

Roots

There's a famous sentiment attributed to Pope Benedict XVI that the Catholic Church should, or at least would, become "smaller and purer." It's held up by the pope emeritus's critics as a sign of his ecclesial myopia and theological closed-mindedness, the kind of thing that earned him the epithet "God's Rottweiler" during his tenure at the Congregation for the Doctrine of the Faith. I'm ashamed to say that I took that characterization at face value upon his election to the papacy: I was practicing the Faith only sporadically in 2005, and after all he *was* German and *did* seem to have a cranky disposition.

I came to see Benedict, as a bumper sticker popular in certain Catholic circles put it, more as a reliable German Shepherd than a temperamental Rottweiler. And I think this was a more accurate representation all along. It turns out that this is nowhere clearer than in the original radio address, from all the way back in 1969, of which that "smaller and purer" sentiment is a crass simplification.

At the end of the 1960s, Benedict was Fr. Joseph Ratzinger, a forty-two-year-old priest and professor at the University of Regensburg. Through most of the decade, including his participation in the Second Vatican Council, Fr. Ratzinger would have been categorized

1

among the more liberal, reform-minded faction in the Church. But as the decade came to a close, the momentum of that faction was taking many of its members outside the bounds of orthodoxy and reason itself, and Ratzinger refused to follow.

It was then, at the close of that tumultuous decade, that the professor was asked to give an address on the future of the Catholic Church for German radio. As confusing and volatile as the third decade of the twenty-first century promises to be, this moment — especially in Germany — may have been the most uncertain since the Protestant Reformation. Indeed, implied in the prompt given to Fr. Ratzinger was the question, "Does the Catholic Church have any future at all?"

The wise professor-priest's words could be applied seamlessly to today's world:

> The future of the Church can and will issue from those whose roots are deep and who live from the pure fullness of their faith. It will not issue from those who accommodate themselves merely to the passing moment or from those who merely criticize others and assume that they themselves are infallible measuring rods; nor will it issue from those who take the easier road, who sidestep the passion of faith, declaring false and obsolete, tyrannous and legalistic, all that makes demands upon men, that hurts them and compels them to sacrifice themselves.[1]

Let's focus first on the concept of "roots." One of my favorite words to describe our age is "deracinated," which comes from

[1] Joseph Ratzinger, *Faith and the Future* (San Francisco: Ignatius Press, 2009). Excerpted in Tod Warner, "When Father Joseph Ratzinger Predicted the Future of the Church," Aleteia, June 13, 2016, https://aleteia.org/2016/06/13/when-cardinal-joseph-ratzinger-predicted-the-future-of-the-church/.

the French for "root," *racine*. For a plant, to be uprooted is to be detached from its means of sustenance—from that which gives it not just life but character. For a dandelion to be pulled up is one thing, but for a mature tree to be uprooted is to devastate an entire ecosystem of coexisting flora and fauna. While something new and beautiful can eventually arise, what has been is gone forever.

The roots of secular culture that have been put down all around us, having violently uprooted the previous culture, are shallow and liable to be pulled up themselves at any moment. If our roots in faith and the authentic tradition of the Church are similarly shallow, then we, as individuals, families, and communities, will be pulled up with them. But if our roots reach and embrace the bedrock of Christ, then we will not only be stable ourselves, but we will be models of confident and joyful stability for others who are looking for something, anything, to hold onto.

The other essential fact about roots is that their purpose is not depth for its own sake, but for the sake of the growth and flourishing of the plant above the soil. Strong roots for a flower that has been strangled or a sapling that has been starved of sunlight are useless: The point is to anchor and sustain something that's living, maturing, developing. A living faith tradition, then, is one that is *both* deeply rooted *and* responsive to the world around it, both anchored in timeless truths and, precisely due to the confidence that comes from that anchoring, eager to innovate.

Smaller

The next aspect of Fr. Ratzinger's address should have been heeded by prelates around the Western world when he gave it. Instead, an irrational optimism too often prevailed, leaving the Church unprepared for the upheavals and contractions to come.

The Prodigal Church

From the crisis of today the Church of tomorrow will emerge
— a Church that has lost much. She will become small and
will have to start afresh more or less from the beginning. She
will no longer be able to inhabit many of the edifices she
built in prosperity. As the number of her adherents dimin-
ishes, so it will lose many of her social privileges. In contrast
to an earlier age, it will be seen much more as a voluntary
society, entered only by free decision.[2]

This last point is absolutely essential to understanding the
Church in twenty-first-century America — and the need for this
book. The culture, both within the Church and in the surrounding society, that sustained generations in a genuine and living
Faith *without them having to think much about it* is gone, for good.
Nearly every Catholic I know of my age — early thirties — is either
a convert or, like myself, a "revert" who spent substantial time away
from the practice of the Faith before making an active decision to
accept the Father's invitation back into the family of faith. While
the Church is not *by nature* a voluntary association — the duties
of baptism bind us whether we like it or not — socially she now
acts like one.

This is not ideal, to say the least. The Church is our supernatural Mother, and we don't choose our mother. But it is reality.
And as with any reality that God allows to come to pass, there
are opportunities.

One of the theses of this book is that, in our families and
friendships and parishes, we should be working toward rebuilding

---

[2] A couple sentences after this, a vestige of Fr. Ratzinger's more radical
liberalism emerged in a prediction of part-time priests: "Undoubtedly [the Church] will discover new forms of ministry and will
ordain to the priesthood approved Christians who pursue some
profession."

a culture where practicing the Faith goes without saying, where it's just *what people do*. But amid the death throes of the old Catholic culture, there is a certain liberation that allows us to think freshly about what a new Catholic culture might look like. Our institutions are collapsing or fading into irrelevance. The old assumptions about the importance of respectability are disappearing. A generation formed neither by enthusiasm for, nor opposition to, the Second Vatican Council is rising. And all of this is happening, at least in part, because the Church-as-voluntary-association is naturally resulting in new blood entering the fold with fresh perspectives.

And those perspectives tend to be invested precisely in the Church's rootedness, her timelessness, her dual anchors in earthly tradition and heavenly transcendence. Because—and you'll pardon my language—why the hell would you embark on this creaking, ancient, barely seaworthy, poorly run ship if you didn't think there was something extraordinary about it—and if you didn't think its otherworldly destination was worth the risk?

Purer?

While Fr. Ratzinger very clearly implied that a smaller Church was on the horizon, he never actually used the word "purer," and he was right not to do so. It is by no means a given that the remnant from this particular spasm in Church history will be holier than what came before—and indeed the assumption that it is would be a mark against it. That's up to each of us to decide.

What Fr. Ratzinger actually said is much more carefully, and wisely, phrased:

The Church will be a more spiritual Church.... It will be hard going for the Church, for the process of crystallization and clarification will cost her much valuable energy. It will make her poor and cause her to become the Church of the meek. The process will be all the more arduous, for sectarian narrow-mindedness as well as pompous self-will will have to be shed. One may predict that all of this will take time.... But when the trial of this sifting is past, a great power will flow from a more spiritualized and simplified Church.

"A more spiritual Church." This doesn't mean, as some would have it, a less active Church, or a more intellectually and politically reserved Church. It's about where the Church, as an institution and as the community of the faithful, places her hope. As we will see, so much of the decline in the American Church can be attributed to a striving for power and respect on the terms of a hostile culture—and not just over the past few decades.

And so if we are to be truly a "purer" Church, we won't aim for that outcome through spiritual self-assuredness and exclusion —that, as Pope Francis often reminds us, is the way of the Pharisees—but through a thoroughgoing spiritual humility and radical inclusion. This isn't about loosening the discipline of the sacraments or the Church's immutable moral teachings, but about simply recognizing, and living as if *everyone* is a potential member of the Body of Christ. In fact, the confidence to go out and preach the fullness of the gospel is itself a fruit of genuine humility, because Christian authenticity never wins us power and influence.

But it does win souls for Christ. In perhaps the most hauntingly prophetic words of the entire address, Fr. Ratzinger describes, without realizing it, our emerging techno-dystopia:

Men in a totally planned world will find themselves unspeakably lonely. If they have completely lost sight of God, they will feel the whole horror of their poverty. Then they will discover the little flock of believers as something wholly new.

They will discover it as a hope that is meant for them, an
answer for which they have always been searching in secret.

Yes, we need to rediscover and revive our ancient tradition. Yes, in
so doing we will uncover the very deepest roots of our civilization.
But, to the world around us, everything we represent will be *new
again*. And we need to embrace that fact, because the Alpha and
the Omega is always ancient and new, always appearing in new
forms and yet always what we were looking for all along. With
Christ within us and shining through us, we can be that hope, that
answer for a searching world.

Home

Fr. Ratzinger, in closing his address fifty years ago, warned us, "And
so it seems certain to me that the Church is facing very hard times.
The real crisis has scarcely begun." We may well wonder if, even
now, the "real crisis" has begun. Are we in the beginning, the
middle, or the end of the Church's faltering response to modernity?
We are not yet given to know what God knows.

But, in truth, it doesn't really matter. Our role in salvation history isn't to obsess over where exactly we stand in that history; it's
to take up our cross and to follow Christ wherever He desires to
lead us. Earlier in the address, Fr. Ratzinger called this our "daily
passion": "Unselfishness, which makes men free, is attained only
through the patience of small daily acts of self-denial. By this daily
passion ... a man's eyes are slowly opened." And what is revealed
to us is nothing more than the completeness of our dependence
on Him.

Dependence goes against the spirit of our age, but every day
more men and women understand the insufficiency and, indeed,
the inhumanity of that spirit. So many of the pathologies and

injustices, personal and social, that contaminate our culture come from that mania for a perfect independence that is, simply, impossible. And it's impossible not just in terms of everyday practicality: It's impossible because it contradicts reality itself, the reality that at every moment we depend on God for everything, including our very existence.

We find peace, then, when we give up warring against reality and embrace that dependence. This is that peace that all long for even if they don't realize it; this is the closest we can get to a real home for our restless immortal souls during our earthly pilgrimage. The Church will be renewed, and so will our civilization, when at every level she acts with the confidence of knowing that she is that home, that place of rest for the weary souls who are floating aimlessly from pleasure to pleasure — or anxiety to anxiety. This is what Fr. Ratzinger prophesied:

> But I am equally certain about what will remain at the end: not the Church of the political cult, which is dead already, but the Church of faith. It may well no longer be the dominant social power to the extent that she was until recently; but it will enjoy a fresh blossoming and be seen as man's home, where he will find life and hope beyond death.

The Church is the true life, the true hope, and the true home of every soul on earth. How we make that reality apparent and appealing in twenty-first-century America is the topic of the rest of this book.

Part 1

How We Got Here

1

Looking Back

The Best of Times

A few years ago, a parish not far from me in suburban Pittsburgh reprinted 1950s-era bulletins as part of celebrating its hundredth anniversary. They became a sensation among my friends, fellow young Catholics passionate about their Faith and the tradition of the Church, because the bulletins depicted a parish experience very different from what most have come to expect today.

The list of Masses was extraordinary, with as many as ten Sunday and six daily liturgies punctuating the entire morning and early afternoon. The number and variety of ministries and societies and sodalities was inspiring: the Holy Name Society and the Knights of Columbus and the various women's guilds and auxiliaries and so on. This was the portrait of spiritually and socially vital parish life.

This parish wasn't alone. In the middle of the last century, there were hundreds more parishes in the Diocese of Pittsburgh than there are today, and each had several weekly and daily Masses and meetings and ministries. The cathedral parish distributed to everyone within its borders cards that advertised seven Sunday Masses, six daily Masses, and Night Prayer every evening. The back of the cards read, in part:

The Prodigal Church

> Five priests in the Cathedral Rectory are anxious to care
> for your spiritual needs. Please feel free to call upon us at
> any time of the day or night, whenever you think we can
> be helpful to you in a spiritual way.

I spoke recently with a Felician teaching nun who remembers the streets of the city's South Side teeming with Catholic schoolchildren; today, she is one of only a few nuns left in the neighborhood, and she encounters more pet dogs than children on the sidewalk. And of seven ethnic parishes that were situated in the twenty-five blocks of the South Side's floodplain, one remains active.

We can pull the camera back and see more evidence that mid-century was the heyday of American Catholicism. In 1944 and 1945, Bing Crosby played a Catholic priest to popular and critical acclaim—one Academy Award win and another nomination—in *Going My Way* and *The Bells of St. Mary's*. A decade later, even the transgressive (though Catholic) Alfred Hitchcock released a film with a hero priest, *I Confess*. And into the mid-1960s the Church still received downright flattering treatment in the portrayal of two martyrs of the English Reformation in *A Man for All Seasons* (St. Thomas More) and *Becket* (St. Thomas Becket).

Meanwhile, from the 1930s through most of the 1950s, all of Hollywood played by the rules of the Hays Code, which was designed by Catholic lay journalist Martin Quigley and Jesuit priest Daniel Lord to support and promote Catholic values. The general principles enshrined in the Code could have been lifted from a catechism:

> No picture will be produced which will lower the moral
> standards of those who see it. Hence the sympathy of the
> audience should never be thrown to the side of crime, wrong-
> doing, evil, *or sin*.

Correct standards of life shall be presented on the screen, subject only to necessary dramatic contrasts.

Law, *natural or human*, should not be ridiculed, nor shall sympathy be created for its violation.[3]

For any institution today, never mind *Hollywood*, even to recognize the reality of "sin" or "correct standards of life" or "natural law," let alone to commit to honoring them, would be, well, heretical. The era of the Hays Code feels like not just another century, but another world.

Finally, the most vivid example of Catholic influence on and presence in our popular culture was Ven. Archbishop Fulton Sheen. He was a media fixture for nearly four decades, beginning with *The Catholic Hour* on NBC radio in 1930, transferring to television with *Life Is Worth Living* in 1952, and finishing with *The Fulton Sheen Program* from 1961 to 1968. He was not a niche figure: The saintly prelate was either broadcast or syndicated on major networks during his entire run, addressed audiences of up to ten million, and won two Emmy Awards.

Sacraments galore! Priests and kids everywhere! Ministries and societies and sodalities, oh my! Silver screen hero priests! Hollywood beholden to Catholic principles! An archbishop in full regalia on prime-time TV! This was it! What else could we ask for?

The Worst of Times?

We only have to look to Archbishop Sheen himself to see that the reality of midcentury American Catholicism was not always as rosy

---

[3] "The Motion Picture Production Code," 1930, emphasis added. The inclusion of "miscegenation" among prohibited sexual content in the code demonstrates how pervasive the sin of racism was in American society and the Church in this era.

as it appears. On his television programs, Sheen was a keen critic of Soviet communism but also a keen observer of the problems in American life: acquisitiveness and materialism and a growing sense, even then, that the demands of religion were antiquated in an age of liberty and prosperity. The archbishop wrote the following in his autobiography, *Treasure in Clay*, published posthumously in 1982:

> There is a tremendous potentiality for sacrifice among the young in this country. Certainly not the least of the difficulties is that the elders are not challenging them. The young people are rebelling against the bourgeois ethos of their parents, who believed in the American way of life, which judged prosperity by material achievements. But one thing that their parents never asked themselves was what they would do with themselves after they had bettered their condition. To some extent, religion fell in with bourgeois ethics. It began to give not theological insights into the meaning of life, but rather psychological and sociological views to accommodate the bourgeois good life to religion.[4]

In other words, material prosperity was not being put in the service of religious duties—for instance, through tithing and almsgiving—but instead, religion was becoming simply one aspect of bourgeois respectability. Going to one of those ten Sunday Masses wasn't broadly understood as a participation in the heaven-on-earth re-presentation of the sacrifice at Calvary, but as *what respectable people do*. And as *what respectable people did* changed markedly in the succeeding decades, so did Catholic practice.

A woman raised in that era described her Catholic upbringing to me as marked by unquestioned Sunday Mass attendance, borderline

[4] Fulton J. Sheen, *Treasure in Clay* (New York: Image Books, 1982), 62–63.

unsettling respect for the person of the priest, regular participation in parish social life, and a home life completely empty of prayer. This is Catholicism as WASP religion: going through the motions (or, more importantly, *being seen* going through the motions) but lacking the real substance of religion as a virtue that permeates life. It is disintegrated, and thus can neither draw us in deeper nor be effectively passed on to others—including and especially children.

Similarly, my father talks about how the social event of the winter season in his 1960s Pittsburgh neighborhood was Christmas midnight Mass at his parish. Each of the boys would ask a girl to accompany him, and they'd all buy corsages and dress as if for a ball. There is a fine line, though, between the Holy Sacrifice of the Mass *playing a social function*, which is part of an integral Catholic culture, and the Holy Sacrifice of the Mass *becoming a social function*—one at which Jesus Christ is just one guest among many. At a certain point, that line was crossed.

We can also see in this Sheen excerpt a generational analysis that should be at once striking and recognizable as we enter the third decade of this century. To the extent the archbishop is taking sides, he is defending the generation that came of age in the 1960s and 1970s—the baby boomer counterculture—and criticizing their parents, many of whom would have been counted among the "Greatest Generation"—the generation of the Hays Code and Bing Crosby. Sheen sees in that seemingly halcyon time a skin-deep Christianity that was merely one aspect of the "American way of life," along with a television to watch *I Love Lucy* and an automatic Chevy Bel Air and a well-stocked bar cart for throwing back Tom Collinses after bridge.

There's nothing inherently wrong with TVs and Chevys and cocktails, but when they become the motivating force of life itself, they have taken on a weight they cannot bear. To the extent the counterculture was a rejection of this "bourgeois" mentality, it was on the right track! But instead of replacing these worldly goods with spiritual ones, it swapped them for worse idols.

Similarly today, Archbishop Sheen's observation rings true in the tension between millennials and their boomer and Gen-X predecessors. In response to all the charges of laziness and entitlement and irresponsibility flung at my fellow millennials, we might ask: Whose responsibility was it to form us in virtue? Intergenerational discord is a two-way street. (As I enjoy observing: no six-year-old ever asked for a "participation trophy"; they are arranged by and for *parents*.) Seeing in millennial and Gen-Z frustration, rebellion, and alienation an opportunity for *evangelization* rather than for mockery will be something we come back to later in this book.

If midcentury truly was the heyday of American Catholicism, then we must say that it was also the triumph of the adjective over the noun — the moment Catholicism went native.

The Deep History

From the very beginning, the Catholic Church had served as a foil for the United States — an institution and set of principles that American institutions and principles were defined *against*. The liberty promised here was to be both political *and* spiritual, from the oppression of monarchy in civil affairs and (in the form of the pope) in ecclesial affairs. American-style republicanism, Founding Fathers and pamphleteers argued, could never coexist with robust Romish influences on these shores.

Prominent historians have christened anti-Catholicism "the deepest bias in the history of the American people"[5] and, more

---

[5] Philip Jenkins, *The New Anti-Catholicism: The Last Acceptable Prejudice* (Oxford, UK: Oxford University Press, 2003), 23.

poetically, "the most luxuriant, tenacious tradition of paranoiac agitation in American history."[6] Black Americans will rightly raise an eyebrow at these characterizations. But we don't have to place the Black and Catholic experiences in competition to observe that the Catholic Church played an outsized and villainous role in the American political imagination from colonial days through at least the early twentieth century.

And Catholics got the message: While there were millions of colonists at the time of the Revolution, the number of Catholics was counted in the tens of thousands, and the number of priests in the dozens. Only three colonies promised full liberty to Catholics: Pennsylvania (founded on Quaker principles of toleration), Maryland (founded by Catholic aristocrats, but intermittently captured by Protestants who reduced Catholic liberties), and Rhode Island (where not a single Catholic lived).

During the nineteenth century, American westward expansion often took on the aspect of an anti-Catholic crusade. The Louisiana Purchase took the French out of the picture, but most of the continent was first settled by Spaniards. Propaganda for the Mexican-American War, which secured all the land north of the Rio Grande (and nearly much more), emphasized the need to make the continent safe for liberty—which meant of the Anglo-Saxon Protestant variety. The largest mass execution in U.S. history occurred during this war, and was of Catholics: the *San Patricios*, Irish American soldiers who defected to Catholic Mexico after being abused in the U.S. Army for their Faith.

This century also brought the first waves of disreputable Catholic immigrants to American shores: Irish first, then Italians and Poles and Slavs, none of whom were originally considered properly "white" or suited to American-style self-government. Racially they

---

[6] Ibid.

were considered crass and impetuous; politically they were considered suspiciously loyal to the habits and principles of the Old World; religiously they were considered backward, superstitious, and frighteningly obedient to hierarchy; economically they were considered, and used as, raw materials to be fed into the machine of industrialization.

The panic these unwashed hordes of popery inspired in bourgeois American society is hard to overstate. The most celebrated cartoonist in American history, Thomas Nast, portrayed bishops as crocodiles—their miters strikingly lined with teeth—menacing good American children in his "American River Ganges." The Church was regularly portrayed as an octopus strangling American institutions; the cartoon "The Papal Octopus" was captioned:

> Romanism is a Monster, with arms of Satanic power and strength, reaching to the very ends of the earth, the arm of superstition crushing the American child, that of subversion crushing the American Flag, that of bigotry crushing the American Public School, that of ignorance crushing the credulous dupe, that of corruption crushing the law of the land, that of greed grasping public moneys, that of tyranny destroying freedom of conscience, freedom of speech, freedom of the press, all over the world.

Catholics remained near the bottom of the social hierarchy even as (and in part because) their numbers began to give them political power. In 1927, when there were two Catholics for every Protestant living in Pittsburgh, the local chamber of commerce's publicity read, "Pittsburgh is so completely Scotch-Irish that if it should be transported to the north of Ireland ... every Orangeman in the region would welcome it as a blood brother." But such documents were not written by or for the working-class Catholics who manned Pittsburgh's mills and factories.

Looking Back

And so, when we think about the Church in America, we are thinking about a group of people who, for the first few centuries of this country's history, were never at home here — and who were regularly reminded by others of this fact. Thus, we are thinking also of an institution that was dedicated to protecting the interests of these people, which often meant acquiescing with American ideas about liberty and the authority of religious institutions in public life.

Entering the Mainstream

It's hard to fault American Catholics, laity or hierarchy, for wanting to become more fully American. It's human nature to desire to be accepted by our peers, and often it must have felt as if the survival of American Catholics depended on it. The question was always: accepted on what, and whose, terms?

This tension has been the primary driver of American Catholic identity and history. Sometimes, as when American prelates either ignored or outright embraced chattel slavery, the results were truly grim. Other times, though, the prudence practiced by the American Church set the stage for one of the most robust flowerings of Catholicism in the modern age, in the form of American urban Catholic enclaves. Every city older than a century has stories of poor Catholic immigrants pooling their wages and talents to build cathedral-style parish churches — all, as the portal to the sumptuous St. Stanislaus Kostka in Pittsburgh reads, *Ad Majorem Dei Gloriam.*

Through it all, American Catholics have consistently tried to demonstrate that the old paranoia about the Papal Octopus is bunk. In the Civil War, the Irish Brigade under the leadership of the irrepressible Thomas Francis Meagher saw some of the most brutal action of the conflict. American Catholic thinkers, such as the nineteenth-century convert Orestes Brownson and, later, the Jesuit cardinal and Vatican II celebrity John Courtney Murray, tried desperately to place American principles within the Catholic tradition (or Catholic principles within the American tradition, as the case may be).

Sometimes this effort took physical form. Sacred Heart Church in the tony Pittsburgh neighborhood of Shadyside was designed and built as a synthesis of Catholicism and American identity. Its founding pastor, Fr. Thomas Coakley, wanted to demonstrate that the Church *belonged* here—specifically in the ritzy neighborhood of the largely Presbyterian industrialists. The eclectic gothic masterpiece features an enormous back window that traces the entire history of the Church in America, from Columbus and the conquistadors to Catholic schools and universities, culminating in a stylized American flag at the highest point of the grandest window in the church.

And yet the thing with paranoia is that it often begins with something real. The teachings and self-understanding of the Catholic Church *do* come into conflict with American principles, even in their most congenial formulations. A country formed by those Catholic ideas—not the least of which is the primacy and uniqueness of the Catholic Church—*would* look radically different from one formed by the principles of eighteenth-century liberalism. This isn't just about "culture war" issues, such as abortion and marriage, or more traditional concerns, such as religious liberty, but also the organization of the economy and the justice owed to workers and the poor and the very purpose of politics itself, the common good. Thomas Nast was a grade-A bigot (the man drew the Irish as apes), but the American-Catholic tension he identified was real.

This isn't a book about politics—there will be time for that another day—so we won't dwell on the details. Let us just say that a frank acknowledgment by Catholics of the tensions between American and Catholic principles of political order is *absolutely not* incompatible with the genuine moral duty of patriotism. The key point is that you don't have to be patriotic on the terms your country's establishment demands: That would have rather serious implications in regimes like Nazi Germany—or, if we're being honest, a regime that has elevated abortion to a fundamental right. To love your mother *through* her alcoholism with tenderness and care for her authentic well-being is the great virtue of piety; to *ignore* her alcoholism out of misguided love is just enabling. The American-Catholic tension is only a somewhat aggravated version of the unease every Christian should feel during our earthly exile. We *do* have a higher loyalty than to any earthly power. We should never feel fully at home, because *we aren't home.* Part of the Christian calling is to *embrace* that tension while trying, in some small way, to transform the slice of the world God has given each one of us into a taste of heaven. It is not about *resolving* that tension once and for all, and certainly not about doing so by conforming our Faith to the world.

More often than not, however, the history of American Catholicism in the twentieth century is one of responding too deferentially to the ingrained fears of our countrymen. I dislike observing this, because it's easy to see why, after generations of abuse, the emergence of Catholicism into the American mainstream was seen as not just desirable, but a tremendous victory! But I'm also not making it up: It's exactly what Archbishop Sheen is describing when he deplores the capture of religion by bourgeois culture.

Though some American Catholics quite liked the ethnic ghettos and the solidarity they inspired, the siren song of the WASPs proved too hard to resist. Suburbanization (ironically fueled at least in part by ethnic and racial prejudices that had long been deployed *against* Catholics) emptied the old neighborhoods; depression, war, and subsequent prosperity broke down some of the old class barriers; and Catholics settled into the bourgeois "American way of life" as, for the first time, something close to full members. We had made it.

It's easy to fixate on what we've lost from that midcentury era of good feelings and on trying to reclaim it. But it was never quite what it seemed—and certainly wasn't what it looks like in retrospect. The subsequent collapse of the newly cozy relationship between Catholicism and American culture demonstrates just how uneasy, and unequal, it was.

Among the WASPs

I really think John Fitzgerald Kennedy was one of the worst things ever to happen to the Church in America. To understand why, though, let's dive a little deeper into the meaning and importance of "bourgeois."

"Bourgeois" is a word primarily associated these days with the Left, either as a highly technical term in Marxist ideology or as a general term of abuse hurled by the young and radical at the old and settled. As Archbishop Sheen uses it, "bourgeois" describes a comfortable, respectable way of being in the world associated with having achieved the stability of the middle class (or above). The bourgeois is sedate, punctual, courteous, and, above all, *practical*.

One of my favorite pieces of writing about Catholic culture is Christopher Dawson's essay "Catholicism and the Bourgeois Mind." The late English writer and historian draws a distinction between the bourgeois spirit and the effusive, ecstatic, unrestrained spirit he associates with baroque Europe: "the type of character which naturally prefers to spend rather than to accumulate, to give rather than to gain." If the prophet of the bourgeois is the economist who forecasts one's future wealth, the prophet of the baroque is the artist (or, well, the actual prophet) who opens new frontiers of shared beauty and truth. The former is inward-facing and "closed," the latter outward-facing and "open":

> The spirit of the Gospel is eminently that of the "open" type which gives, asking nothing in return, and spends itself for others. It is essentially hostile to the spirit of calculation,

the spirit of worldly prudence and above all to the spirit of religious self-seeking and self-satisfaction. For what is the Pharisee but a spiritual bourgeois, a typically "closed" nature, a man who applies the principle of calculation and gain not to economics but to religion itself, a hoarder of merits, who reckons his accounts with heaven as though God was his banker? It is against this "closed," self-sufficient moralist ethic that the fiercest denunciations of the Gospels are directed. Even the sinner who possesses a seed of generosity, a faculty of self-surrender, and an openness of spirit is nearer to the kingdom of heaven than the "righteous" Pharisee; for the soul that is closed to love is closed to grace.

Dawson identifies the bourgeois and antibourgeois spirits with Protestantism and Catholicism respectively, which can be seen to this day in the cultural geography of the West. German-inflected Protestant nations remain economical, practical, unemotional. Mediterranean Catholic nations practice siestas and hours-long café breaks, and they never arrive anywhere on time. My sister's visit to a restaurant in Athens—influenced by the similarly effusive spirit of the Eastern Church—ended with everyone dancing on the tables and no one paying.

The United States had been something of a battleground between the sedate and calculating bourgeois, in the form of the WASP establishment, and the precocious and sometimes chaotic antibourgeois, in the form of teeming Catholic ghettos. Just as much as fear of political-ecclesial takeover, this culture clash motivated concerns about Catholic influence here. And it was overcoming these concerns that led American Catholics to mimic more or less WASP cultural habits after entering the mainstream.

And what is WASPier than running for president? The rise of Kennedy represented the final step in the welcoming of Catholicism

The Prodigal Church

into American life. We weren't just winning and running Midwest cities through violence and corruption — or, uh, service and solidarity — anymore: We had (more or less) respectably climbed the mountain and had our boy in the White House. But, we ask again, on whose terms?

On the campaign trail in 1960, the Massachusetts senator was invited to speak about his faith to the Greater Houston Ministerial Association. He reassured the Protestant ministers in attendance: "I believe in a president whose religious views are his own private affair." He continued:

> I do not speak for my church on public matters, and the church does not speak for me. Whatever issue may come before me as president — on birth control, divorce, censorship, gambling or any other subject — I will make my decision … in accordance with what my conscience tells me to be the national interest, and without regard to outside religious pressures or dictates. And no power or threat of punishment could cause me to decide otherwise.[7]

These were the terms of admittance to the White House, and thus the terms of full admittance to American life: One could be a baptized, confirmed, Mass-going Catholic, but that could not possibly come with any responsibilities outside the "private" sphere. Kennedy is describing here Catholicism as little more than a hobby, a club membership, maybe at most a kind of identity. But it is completely, explicitly private: We could be fully American Catholics, but outside the four walls of the church, and maybe the home, we had to resolve all tensions in favor of secular-Protestant America.

---

[7] John F. Kennedy, "Speech to the Greater Houston Ministerial Association," September 12, 1960, National Public Radio, transcript, https://www.npr.org/templates/story/story.php?storyId=16920600.

Looking Back

Kennedy became, of course, a sensation among American Catholics in a way not unlike the way Barack Obama was regarded by Black Americans. He was the symbol of our progress, of our acceptance, even of our maturation into full members of the community. His portrait was placed in Catholic homes next to the Holy Father's. When he died, he was mourned as something like a martyr.

But the lesson he symbolized was that to be fully American, we couldn't be fully Catholic — and that this was a sacrifice worth making. The evidence of subsequent years is that the lesson was learned well.

Swept Away

It was in this context that the Second Vatican Council played out. And it is important simply to remember that the council *did* have a context: It was called as a response to real troubles for the Church, and it took place within real history. Both champions and skeptics of the council tend to speak as if it were an incursion into the life of the Church, either as a second revelation or as the work of a cabal of infiltrators. The truth is that it was the work of real men responding to real problems guided by the real Holy Spirit.

(That doesn't mean we should engage the work of the council, and especially its reception, uncritically. But we'll get to that in a minute.)

Notwithstanding the gilded portrait of midcentury Catholicism sketched at the beginning of this chapter, the Church in America and around the world was not in the best of health. The bourgeois spirit described by Archbishop Sheen, for instance, was both reflected in and exacerbated by rote, uninspiring liturgical praxis. Remember those jam-packed Sunday Mass schedules? Well, if you're having Masses every hour on the hour, they're lasting a lot less than an hour. This could become, and often did become, a sacramental assembly line: get 'em in; get 'em out; get 'em going.

This isn't *necessarily* bad! There's a beautiful efficiency in maximizing the distribution of sacramental grace. (I certainly wouldn't mind having to wrangle our four children for a forty-minute Sunday Mass now and again.) But at a certain point rushed and casual approach to liturgy seeps into the faithful as a rushed and casual approach to prayer and the life of faith generally. It signals that this weekly ritual is that and only that—a box to check and a place to be seen on the way to more important activities.

And so the question of how the Church was to speak to this modern and rapidly changing world was an important one. In substantial ways, the prevailing way of doing business was not working, and the Church felt adrift. She is at her best when she asserts timeless truths in a manner and tenor well calibrated to the culture she is engaging; now, perhaps in the most serious way since the French Revolution, she no longer understood what that culture needed, or even what it was.

I can't imagine what it must have been like to live through the Second Vatican Council. Thank goodness it occurred before the days of the Internet and social media: The competing minute-by-minute reports that emerge from even minor Vatican events these days are enough to drive a person mad. If a pope calls another ecumenical council in my lifetime, I might smash all my screens to bits and retire to a mountaintop in West Virginia. But even in the days of newsprint and radio and a little television, the regular updates and expectations and prognostications must have been unbearably disorienting.

The book you are reading is *not* a Vatican II book. It is, in fact, anything but a Vatican II book. So let's make just a few observations that should be relatively uncontroversial. First, more seemed to be on the table than had been since at least the early dogmatic councils—and more than actually was on the table. The possibility of *impossibly* radical changes, even though they didn't come to pass, destabilized both those who hoped for them and those who feared them.

Second, the way the faithful *experienced* the Church *did* change radically, and seemingly overnight. This had a much greater impact on the average layperson than the (arguably) modest theological adjustments in the council's long and rather involved documents. Students left school one spring, and returned the next fall to habit-less nuns and a whitewashed chapel. Altars were unceremoniously ripped out of walls and ancient relics stored in basements, where many languish to this day. Folk bands, such as the hippie-themed Peacemakers that played at the parish in our Pittsburgh neighborhood, appeared as if conjured by Scott McKenzie himself.

Third, the *overall impression* given by the overeager news media, the overzealous liturgists, and the often downright mendacious clergy and hierarchy, was that *everything had changed*. Sure, the doctrine was still more or less intact, but the Church had come of age. She had caught up to the rest of the world, and we could finally say we were Catholic without a hint of apology in our voices. And whatever she hadn't yet come to her senses on—birth control, for instance—she would soon. (Surprise!)

But—and here's the important point—the notion that the Church had really fully embraced the modern world, and specifically the very *Americanized* modern world, did not *just* come from the council, its documents, and its reception. It had been seeded years before in the words and actions of the faithful and many members of the hierarchy who had embraced the bourgeois American way of life as fully compatible with Catholicism. In the 1950s, even though the Church was *liturgically* Tridentine, she was increasingly *socially* and *spiritually* postconciliar—a decade ahead of time. The council, then, represented a culmination of a decades-long process just as much as it launched the new reality of the postconciliar Church.

The thing about being in the mainstream is that when the river changes course, so do you—until you gather up the strength and the boldness to climb out. The American Church has been in the current for a long time now, and it affects just about every aspect of the way we think about faith and life itself. We need to understand the implications of this status quo before we can understand the challenges—and the opportunities—moving forward.

2

The Prodigal Church

Dissipation

> After a few days, the younger son collected all his belong-
> ings and set off to a distant country where he squandered
> his inheritance on a life of dissipation. When he had freely
> spent everything, a severe famine struck that country, and
> he found himself in dire need. (Luke 15:13–14, NAB)

It's the parable of the prodigal son, of course. And it's our story, too.

Now, if the boy had simply spurned his parents, it would have been impious—a violation of the virtue of piety by which we honor the order of creation and the sacrifices others have made for us. But he goes further: He takes his inheritance, *then* leaves. The prodigal son demands the trappings of adulthood, *then* behaves like a child. He accepts his father's generosity, *then* rejects his authority.

I've always been impressed by the word used to describe the young man's wastefulness: The New American Bible takes the word directly from the Latin Vulgate—*dissipavit*, "dissipated." It's a wonderfully evocative word, bringing to mind innumerable ex-amples from the physical world to illustrate the moral principle. I like to think of the sandcastle being lapped, then eroded, then overtaken by the tide.

The Prodigal Church

What distinguishes dissipation is its permanence. A broken bone can be mended; a shattered vase, even if broken into a thousand pieces, can at least theoretically be restored. In dissipation, however, the very principle of a thing's integrity is lost and cannot be recovered. It is unrecognizable as what it once was. It is indistinguishable from its environment.

For the prodigal son, the dissipation of his inheritance also represented the dissipation of his very self, the loss of his integrity as a person. It began with the initial act of rupture, disintegrating the family who raised and loved him and lacerating his relationship with God. Then it continued with "loose living," as another translation puts it, as his control over himself deteriorated and the flesh took the reins from the spirit. And finally he is completely dissipated, his inheritance in money and morals eroded down to nothing, unrecognizable as the happy boy of his youth and indistinguishable from the cruel and crass world around him.

This is, I submit, an image of the Catholic Church in America in the twenty-first century.

As we stressed in the last chapter, this isn't just about Vatican II, or even modernism or liberalism or any other single and simple scapegoat. And it's not this stark in every region and institution: The Church is, by any measure, thriving in pockets of grace-filled authenticity.

Furthermore, to the diminishing extent the world around us remains righteous, the dissipation of the Church and her patrimony can take place without much notice. This is how entering the mainstream of American life proceeded in the twentieth century: Ten Sunday Masses at suburban parishes could (seem to) coexist comfortably with embracing the bourgeois spirit because Bing Crosby in a cassock was winning Oscars.

But that dissipation looks much less favorable — and more noticeable — when the environment declines further into a secular anti-morality. Even more importantly, though: *This is not the Church's calling.* Christ exhorted His followers to be salt and light, bringing the flavor and radiance and warmth of grace to a fallen world. And should we allow the salt to lose its taste, to lose its ability to bring welcome change to the world and instead be dissipated into meaninglessness? "It is no longer good for anything except to be thrown out and trodden under foot by men." (Matt. 5:13) This holds regardless of how many bishops are on prime-time television.

When times were good, the prodigal son could skate by. His life might not have been ideal, but it seemed sustainably *good enough*. But then the famine struck.

Famine

Integrity is the quality of wholeness or completeness that permits a thing, group, or person to fulfill its purpose. We say a building has integrity when it can withstand the regular stresses of its use and environment. We say the same about a community of integrity—that it is free of the kind of discord that weakens bonds and threatens longevity. And we say a person has integrity when he says what he means and means what he says, when there is a unity among thoughts and words and actions that emanates peace.

Jesus Christ is the exemplar of integrity. Not only is He a man of perfect honesty and perfect righteousness, but He is the perfect union of divinity and humanity, containing both within Himself in their fullness. Thus He *effected* integrity in others, and through grace continues to do so. There is no integrity more important than union with Christ, where all our personal and social (and even, in a sense, architectural) integrity is rooted. And the most beautiful truth of all is that the integrity Christ offers us is not merely mimicry of Him, but true union with Him, and ultimately transformation into Him.

The Prodigal Church

In this integrity are strength and solidity, and thus the ability to withstand confusion and crisis. The well-constructed building gives us shelter from storms and tremors. The durable community gives us material and spiritual support when the order around it convulses. The person at peace with himself and his God has an anchor of truth and love when the relevance of both is tested by an emergency.

The prodigal son, after his "life of dissipation," lacked the material, social, and personal stability of integrity when the famine descended. He was completely vulnerable. The famine — a fearful prospect even for the most well-positioned members of the community — is for him a death sentence.

The Church in the twenty-first century finds herself confronting a spiritual famine, while at the same time struggling with a crisis of integrity as serious as any she has faced in her earthly history. She is perceived not just by the world but very often by the faithful as merely one institution among many in the American scene, a competitor in the "marketplace of (religious) ideas." Her value to the world is not well understood, even by some of those who direct her earthly course. She cannot die, but her witness can be smothered, and thus her purpose frustrated.

And the most tragic thing of all is this: It is in the famine that we need her most.

Faded Flavor

What does it mean, though, to say that the Church has dissipated her distinctiveness? I hope you'll forgive me for finding an analogy in one of my hobbies: golf.

When you think about golf tournaments, what's the first one that comes to mind? I bet for most it's the Masters, the annual rite of spring hosted with uncanny precision by the Augusta National Golf Club. And for good reason! The club invests an incredible amount of time and energy to preserve its aura as a place set apart from the troubles of the world, a veritable gated paradise where neither a blade of grass nor a bloom of azalea is out of place.

This extends especially to the television presentation of the tournament. The club has insisted (successfully) that CBS commentators be sacked for what would normally be considered minor missteps, such as referring to the spectators—excuse me, *patrons*—as a "mob." The limited-commercial broadcasts are always sponsored by the most enduring stars in the corporate firmament: companies like IBM, AT&T, ExxonMobil, and Mercedes-Benz. Even promos for other CBS programs are banned.

By ensuring startling consistency not just in what's directly within its control—the appearance of the tournament and the golf course—but also in the public's interface with the club—through wielding its clout with broadcasters—Augusta National has preserved and embraced its distinctiveness. This is an incredible achievement in today's world, which insists on flattening and commodifying, reducing everything interesting to just another example of a type: just another sporting event, just another television broadcast, just another weekend distraction. But who could deny that even now Augusta National and the tournament it hosts are not just *different* but *special*?

What a tragedy it is, then, that around the country the Catholic Church and her institutions have failed to project the most basic quality of *specialness*. Our institutional heritage has been reduced to just another university, just another charity, or just another religious organization. The Church—the very Body of Christ in this world, the mediator of all grace to humanity, the perfect heavenly society of the saints and angels—has acquiesced to the steamroller.

Here's a minor example, also from the world of sports: Not to pick exclusively on the nation's flagship Catholic university, but you could watch a Notre Dame football game on television without

33

getting any more than a faint notion that the university is Catholic. We could imagine a pregame Hail Mary (the real kind) that the university insists NBC broadcast, but nope: Notre Dame has at least as much cultural and financial clout as Augusta National, but its identity has been reduced to a *brand*, a *fandom* to rally around, almost completely emptied of *substance*. Augusta National brings to mind obsessive, borderline creepy aesthetic perfection, and that's exactly what it's going for. Notre Dame brings to mind leprechauns and *Rudy* and Touchdown Jesus—Christ Himself reduced to an aspect of the football brand—and I suppose that's exactly what it's going for.

On the one hand, the example of Notre Dame is merely a symptom of a timid and often apologetic approach to Catholic identity that pervades American Catholicism. On the other hand, it's also, in some small way, a cause of the perpetuation of this timidity. When the everyday faithful, with much less power and capacity for risk than a major university, see such institutions failing to project a confidently Catholic public image, why should we be surprised when they keep their Faith safely private, and their images safely respectable, their public convictions safely lukewarm?

That is, certainly, what has happened. When public pollsters break down their data by religion, on every topic from abortion to foreign affairs to the economy, the views of self-described Catholics have converged with those of the general population. While the views of Mass-going Catholics, as opposed to all self-identified Catholics, generally align more closely with Church teaching, at least on hot-button "culture war" issues, this doesn't let us off the hook. The fact that so many people call themselves Catholic while feeling no particular duty to live and think as Christians demonstrates just how much the Church has become merely an identity or a brand, rather than an encounter with divinity in the Person of Jesus Christ.

I want to be absolutely clear: This observation about the dissipation of our political and cultural witness *is not* about any perceived capitulation to "the Left" or to limp notions of "social justice." (If anything, we need a greater emphasis on authentic and comprehensive social justice, highlighting the criminalization of abortion *and* the need for humane immigration policies, the promotion of genuine marriage *and* the living wage, all as essential, interconnected elements of a just society.) Rather, it is clear in polling and public discourse that we identify Catholic teaching far too easily with doctrinaire progressivism *or* conservatism. We've been dissipated into partisan and ideological tribes instead of demonstrating a better way—the way of integrity.

Another aspect of the Church's public face that has undergone a certain dissipation is her public prayer: the liturgy. Unlike more radical traditionalists, I want to insist that the Ordinary Form of the Mass does not have to be banal. The fact that it *is* so often banal is not a necessary result of Vatican II, but rather its betrayal. Indeed, some of the most transporting Masses I've ever attended are those that hewed most faithfully to the rubrics of Pope St. Paul VI.

We don't need to go into the specifics of liturgical aesthetics to say that the Mass should be clearly an occasion, and the church clearly a place, *set apart from the ordinary*. Dissipation occurs when the Church acquiesces to the surrounding culture—such as, for instance, in embracing casualness, iconoclasm, and musical forms that, frankly, have more in common with Broadway than traditional sacred music—rather than co-opts and elevates the surrounding culture. As salt and light, we are not supposed to melt into the world and become indistinguishable from it, but rather we are to transform it, to make it more beautiful, more *human*, than it was before. We meet people where they are not to have a little party, but to lift them to planes of holiness they might not have thought attainable.

The Prodigal Church

Just as important as the Mass itself, though, are other aspects of liturgical life. The fading away of the liturgical calendar is one of the most striking examples of the modern American Church's squandering of our inheritance—and the growing movement to restore its place one of our most hopeful trends. Growing up in suburban Pittsburgh, I was really aware of only those feast days that had been co-opted into secular holidays: St. Patrick's Day and St. Valentine's Day—and I didn't even know Valentine's Day grew out of a Catholic feast.

There is one exception, though: the feast of St. Blaise. The day's traditional throat blessing was a fixture of my childhood. I remember being a little afraid to approach the priest and expose my neck to the crossed candles. (It required a small act of vulnerability, which enhances trust, as we'll discuss later.) But it's precisely the *differentness* of the throat blessing, the fact that it was a little weird and a little mysterious and, yes, a little frightening, that made it such a memorable act of openness to God's action in our lives. It's dispiriting how few of those moments, outside of Communion itself, we have left.

The point of making the life of the Church more accessible to modern sensibilities—simpler, less mysterious, less otherworldly—was to bring the life-giving, elevating, and perfecting grace of Christ to more people. It was, at its best and most sincere, an attempt to renew the Church through authentic innovation. It failed—there's no better word for the sad outcome—in part because it became too committed to an ideology of tradition and too detached from creativity.

That might sound surprising, but let me explain.

The New Traditionalism

The Catholic Church doesn't change quickly, and that's generally a good thing. But when the world around her does change quickly, and demands a new and thoughtful response, she's rarely on her toes. The Church's response to totalitarianism, for instance, focused initially on finding common ground and securing her liberty and other interests, as symbolized in the 1933 concordat with Nazi Germany. It took until 1937 — reflecting, to be fair, lightning speed in Church terms — for Pope Pius XI to condemn German pagan-atheistic totalitarianism in his encyclical *Mit Brennender Sorge* ("With Burning Concern").

The implementation of Vatican II, itself arguably a *tardy* response to the challenges of modernity, represented a radically new and dynamic pace of change for the Church. It was destabilizing, as we've said, but also an exciting opportunity for real creativity and genuine innovation within tradition. But old habits quickly kicked in, and tradition became calcified. The thing was that the stagnant tradition was the *new* one, the one born in the 1960s.

A story may help to illustrate. A few years ago, not far from where I live, there was a "listening session" for young adults held by the diocese as part of its restructuring. Helmed by a permanent deacon from a suburban parish, the event was billed as a forum for feedback from the twenty-somethings of the region about how the Church could serve them better. To this end, participants were encouraged to submit questions on index cards. One question, read aloud by the facilitator, went like this:

> Young people love tradition. What can be done to create more options for traditional liturgy (Latin, *ad orientem*, etc.) in the diocese?

Immediately after finishing the question, the deacon disputed the premise that young people were drawn to more traditional liturgical forms. Then, his countenance brightening, he talked about the new drum set his parish had just purchased, and how the musical opportunities it created would draw young people. Finally, as an afterthought, he suggested that incorrigible traditionalists could frequent the diocese's sole Latin-Mass community.

Now, there are lots of things one might say in response to this anecdote, some more charitable than others. Let me suggest, however, that the young adults were being patronized by stagnant, uncreative, backward-thinking traditionalism. The deacon's imagination was constrained by *what had been* and could not grasp *what could be*. And *what has been* for the past few generations is a continual and often quite pathetic attempt to keep up with secular culture.

Put more starkly: For the generation of laity and clergy who now dominate the Church's bureaucracy and hierarchy, drum sets *are traditional*. "On Eagle's Wings" and "Gift of Finest Wheat" are traditional. Round churches with highly abstract stained glass windows are traditional. Extraordinary ministers of Holy Communion and Communion in the hand are traditional. The restoration of deeper traditions, on the other hand, is a frightening innovation that threatens the new tradition. This "new traditionalism" is especially strong because the generation in question either actively ushered in the new tradition or received it in childhood, and thus feels ownership over it.

The new traditionalism manifests itself especially in denial. A priest friend suggested to me that dioceses should have begun planning for decline the moment Catholic birth rates significantly dropped, and who could disagree? Instead, after decades or even generations of irresponsible and unrealistic optimism, dioceses especially in low-immigration regions are frantically closing parishes and merging schools—all temporary, even if necessary, fixes, as we will discuss. The theory was that if we could just stay in the mainstream, if we could just maintain the respectability we had achieved in midcentury, everything would eventually be alright.

But it wouldn't. And it won't.

The Prodigal Church

Addled Imagination

The prevailing assumption in the American Church is that we're still working out the implications of the Second Vatican Council. Everything good and bad about the modern Church gets traced back to the council and its implementation and reception. But that's short sighted and implicitly accepts the new-traditionalist framing that everything that matters began in the 1960s.

No, I think that, at least in this country, we're still working out the implications of the Church's midcentury embrace of the American way of life. How we imagine what the Church is and can be is hemmed in by our addiction to respectability, by our immersion in the mainstream. And just as a fish can't imagine walking on land, we can't imagine being anywhere else.

To the extent Vatican II failed in its project of renewal, then, we can blame a *preexisting* suspicion of Catholic distinctiveness and obsession with cultivating and maintaining hard-won respectability. For instance, the new form of the Mass was surely designed in part to appeal to lower-church Protestants, which certainly could have been a noble step toward unity, but in our enthusiasm for WASP normalcy, parishes too often downright mimicked their rites. It might have been possible for the postconciliar American Catholic Church to have remained confident in her distinctive identity, but that would have required the preexisting gumption to do so. And it wasn't there.

To this day our assumption that we *must belong*, that *by right* we are and must remain in the American mainstream, is the highest barrier we face to genuine renewal. It discourages us from making bold claims about the reality of Christ, the Church, the sacraments, and our common life. It discourages us from public prayer, from talking about Jesus with others, even from displaying religious articles in our homes, lest we seem strange or lowbrow. (My friends' rather posh realtor insisted that they remove their crucifixes and other religious artwork when "staging" their home for sale, observing that buyers would be put off.)

It discourages us from embracing our ancient traditions and applying them in creative ways to our times. In other words, it discourages us from being the signs of contradiction we're called to be.

Our imaginations are so restricted by our desire for respectability that we struggle to see not only *what can be*, but *what is*. The reality is that God is in control, that His Church is the unique means of our salvation, that He calls us to love our enemies and to evangelize the world, that grace is real and transformative, and that holiness is the most important thing we can pursue in this life. None of this is respectable. Each of these truths impinges in some way on our culture's bourgeois materialism, its practical relativism, its lust for autonomy and control, its abhorrence of universal claims and duties, its terror of meekness and vulnerability.

Each of these cultural pathologies requires an entire book of its own. For our purposes, however, let us just say that the first step toward tackling them is to recognize them. And the first step toward recognizing them is overcoming our own terror of transgressing respectability, our own terror of being recognizably different.

Because it's impossible to get Church renewal right if we don't understand what the Church *is* in God's order. And it's impossible to break new ground in Catholic family and community life if we don't understand what families and friendships *are meant for*. Much of the rest of this book will be about recovering those basic truths so we can understand how to make the Church, her institutions, and all the relationships that comprise them the best they can be in our time. Achieving this will require an understanding of what we'll call authentic innovation.

Authentic Innovation

The argument of this chapter is that we have dissipated our distinctive traditions in order to please the surrounding culture, but have lost both our patrimony and our position in the process. But that doesn't mean the solution is mimicking or re-creating a particular time in the Church's history, whether the 1950s or the 1250s. There's no bringing back the good old days—and, as we've emphasized, they weren't as good as we like to think.

But the deeper problem with this archaeological approach, where we try to piece together hints of *how things were* and bring them back to life, is that it misunderstands what tradition is and what makes a tradition vital. Traditions—even sacred Tradition—are dynamic. They exist in and through time, adapting to circumstances, changing through the choices of the human beings who live within them. They are anchored in timeless truths, rooted in past experiences, informed by accumulated wisdom in the here and now, and—crucially—oriented toward the future.

Attempts to recreate a particular moment in the past aren't acts of authentic traditionalism any more than Renaissance Fairs are. A tradition that can imagine only *how things were* but not *how things could be* is not a tradition at all, but a reenactment. And when we mistake that kind of role-playing for the real thing, we embrace a corpse, while ignoring our duty to keep genuine, living traditions alive.

This *does not* mean that reviving lost or moribund traditions is necessarily counterproductive. The important thing is that the re-creation can't be an end in itself. To take up a potent example, the freedom to celebrate the Mass of 1962—the Traditional Latin Mass (TLM), the Extraordinary Form, the Tridentine Mass, whatever you want to call it—is a valuable part of keeping the deep liturgical tradition of the Church alive. But the tradition becomes stagnant, and thus not really a tradition at all but rather a kind of playacting, if the community's purpose is just slavishly to enact the 1962 rubrics forever.

Vital, genuine traditionalism will embrace local variations and organic changes, so long, of course, as they adhere to the internal logic of the tradition. And the ultimate goal for TLM communities must be to make a liturgy in the spirit of that tradition, *but not necessarily the precise Mass of 1962 or 1954 or any other point in time*, the everyday form of the Mass once again. This is accomplished by forming welcoming, dynamic communities of faith dedicated *first* to holiness (especially in the form of docility to God's will) and only secondarily to liturgical precision.

Authentic innovation, then, is about neither simply bringing back the past nor experimenting willy-nilly as if the past didn't happen. It's about plumbing the depths of our tradition — the early Church *and* the monastics *and* the Middle Ages *and* the Counter-Reformation *and* modern social teaching *and* the experience of the past few generations — and applying that tradition in a forward-thinking way to the particular circumstances of the twenty-first century. That might mean reembracing liturgical forms that respond to the contemporary craving for order and authenticity. It might also mean reembracing decentralized diocesan and parochial authority in response to contemporary realities in staffing and resources.

Above all, it means understanding once again the fact that our God is the only God, our Christ the only Christ, and our Church the only Church. We affirm this in the Creed at every Mass, but too often speak and act as if God and Christ and the Church are each one among many. We talk about what "my Church" or "my religion" requires of me (and only me) instead of what "*the* Church" and "*true* religion" require of everyone. And we give that Church and the God she serves only the leftovers of our time and means and attention, not the first claim.

Only in coming back to reality can we renew the Church. Only in knowing what the reality of the Church and the parish and the family and the person is *in God's eyes* can we pursue innovation with authenticity, breaking free of the chains of respectability while remaining anchored to timeless truth.

But more than *understanding* this reality, we have to *desire* to live it out. Conversion is the prerequisite of renewal.

Reconciliation

The thing with dissipation is that it makes restoration impossible. There's no earthly way to reconstitute a swept-away sandcastle with the original grains. It's gone.

And that's why our situation can often seem so hopeless. It's why, I believe, so many Catholics are gravitating toward answers that are unavailable to us: sweeping away unpalatable truths about sexuality and the priesthood and the authority of the hierarchy—and the piety we owe our spiritual fathers regardless of our feelings toward them. Maybe I spend too much time on Twitter, but there seems to be an overwhelming feeling that nothing good can come from the institutional Church in our day.

But if the prodigal son never stopped wallowing in the pigsty, he would've died there. And so do we court spiritual death by despairing of the possibility of the reconstitution of our patrimony. Because the truth is that there is One who can restore even the most seemingly hopeless dissipation: The Father can make us whole again, as individuals and as a Church. It's up to us to accept the invitation. And the first step is realizing what we've given up.

> But when he came to himself he said, "How many of my father's hired servants have bread enough and to spare, but I perish here with hunger! I will arise and go to my father, and I will say to him, 'Father, I have sinned against heaven and before you; I am no longer worthy to be called your son; treat me as one of your hired servants.'" (Luke 15:17–19)

The prodigal son had to come to his senses to accept the reality that his dissipation had left him helpless and that his father had the answer. More than that, he had to trust not only that his father *could* help him, but that he *would*.

Too often our projects of renewal are based on our own methods and wisdom. Diocesan programs are regularly laid out in Power-Points and flowcharts that are indistinguishable from the products of corporate committees. They're shot through with corporate clichés like "resource management" and "measurable outcomes," and sometimes the new jargon of Silicon Valley—"disruption" and other concepts that make donors smile while leaving everybody else confused and demoralized. Concepts like prayer and grace and holiness are reduced to bit players or, maybe worse, inclusion among the "measurables."

This is not the way of the gospel. Our prodigal Church, having dissipated her inheritance, needs *first* to trust in the healing power of the Father's grace, love, and mercy. After all, this is what He wants more than anything:

> But the father said to his servants, "Bring quickly the best robe, and put it on him; and put a ring on his hand, and shoes on his feet; and bring the fatted calf and kill it, and let us eat and make merry; for this my son was dead, and is alive again; he was lost, and is found." And they began to make merry. (Luke 15:22–24)

The boy had shattered the integrity of his family and his very being, but his father immediately restores it. In conforming himself to his father's loving will, the boy is healed, and so are his relationships—until, of course, the elder brother goes *his* own way out of pride.

We, too, find our purpose and perfection in allowing Christ to conform us to His will and His very self; thus we become who God made us to be. And the same goes for our families and communities, our parishes and the entire Church: These fulfill their purposes best when they are radically open to grace, thus becoming what He made them to be—mediums of that salvific grace for the entire world. We just need to trust that in seeking first the true, the good, and the beautiful—that is, in seeking first holiness—we will honor God and in turn be blessed by Him.

Everything else is despair, trying the same boring strategies over and over because we lack hope in God's goodness. We chase trends and dilute the Faith and compromise our consciences because the only hope we can muster is in the worldly salvation of popularity, a mainstream respectability that keeps the Church lukewarm but safe—though decreasingly so. We loiter in the pigsty because it's all we've known, and we just don't think the Father can or wants to make us whole.

Moving Forward

That's a stark portrait of the status quo in the American Church. The rest of this book, from time to time, will meditate on these problems in greater detail. But most of it will be about sketching a positive, beautiful portrait of Catholic reality—of *what is* and, therefore, *what can be* if only we let God's grace work in and through us.

Because the time is just right. We have been living in a culture of artifice for some time now, but the veil is slipping more than ever. There's a growing understanding among everyday men and women that *something is not right*, that the modern world we've been sold isn't all it's cracked up to be. This is naturally accompanied by confusion and not a little anger, some of which may be channeled into dangerous social and political movements. People are looking for big solutions to big problems, and big answers to big questions.

This is our moment—if only we have the godly confidence to seize it by embracing the transcendent, incandescent authenticity of the Cross. In Christ Crucified we have the truth that resolves confusion, the peace that resolves anger, the Person who fulfills every human longing. But we have to bring Him to the people and make Him credible through our personal conduct and the institutions we build.

Christ always stood out from the crowd, not because He was tall or physically attractive, not because He was loud or assertive, and not because He promised comfort and wealth and power. No, He stood out because, for those with eyes to see, in every moment and in every aspect of His being He demonstrated who He was. He didn't act like the Son of God with the apostles and then become genteel and inoffensive in public. He didn't speak the language of faith to His friends and the language of the world to strangers. And He certainly didn't harangue the weak and flatter the powerful.

We, too, as individual Catholics and as families, as communities, as the entire Church, can stand out from the crowd in the same way. But it will require the same holy consistency—or consistent holiness—that made Christ a completely, undeniably authentic witness to truth.

While this process begins as part of the spiritual battle waged in every soul, we will begin our description of renewal at the highest level: the institutional Church, whose credibility not just as a witness to Christ but as His very Body is essential to sparking a new springtime for His people.

Part 2

The Church

3

The Visible Church

Be Yourself

"Be yourself": It's the most hackneyed piece of advice there is. And yet there's wisdom in it — if we understand it rightly.

Let's start with that first word. What does it mean "to be"? No, this isn't a trick question: It's important for understanding, well, everything.

We usually think of "being" as passive. It's just existing, and we don't have to *do* anything to exist. Sure, our hearts have to pump blood, and our brains have to generate electrical signals for us to stay alive, but we don't have to take any conscious action simply to be.

But there's a lot more to being than just *sitting there*. We inherit that passive understanding of being from modern scientific materialism, which insists that it's irrational to believe in a Creator, but completely sensible to say that the reason anything exists at all is that it just does, and always has. That kind of existentialism, which drove so many twentieth-century thinkers to despair, has never been the Christian view. It's simply incompatible with the truth of an all-loving Creator.

For the Christian, to be is, first of all, a gift. And a gift has to be received. To exist, then, is to be in a continuous state of receptivity, of receiving the grace of being. That means that being implies relationship — an unbreakable connection between the Creator and His creation. While we may fall out of the *state of grace* through mortal sin, we are not annihilated, even though God could zap us out of existence if He wished.

Part of what it means to exist, then, is to be open to God. And the more receptive we are to God, the more we allow His being to flow in and through us, the more alive we are — the more we just *are*. This may sound strange to us, as we're accustomed to thinking of existence as an all-or-nothing proposal, but again this is a mistaken modern notion. The Christian view of ontology (that's a fancy word for the study of the nature of being) is that all existence comes from God, and all creation participates in being in different ways and at different levels. And so we can grow or recede in being through our openness to Him.

This truth places the "be yourself" cliché in a different light. Because just as "to be" is comprehensible only in relation to God, so too are *you*. To be yourself truly is to be radically open to God's life, grace, and providence. In that way, He makes us who we were meant to be: images of Himself, all while maintaining our wonderful particularity. And so there is nothing better or more fulfilling any human being can hope to be than beautifully, fearfully, transcendently himself.

As this is true for each person, so is it true for the Church, the Body of Christ. She is most herself when she is completely open to God's grace, allowing her to transform herself — both in her institutions and in the faithful who comprise her — into a living icon of the living God. As we will discuss in the next chapter, there are aspects of the Church that are timeless and unchanging; but in her visible, earthly form she exists in time and is responsive to, and responsible for, human realities. This means — as we all know unless we've been living as holy hermits for the last few decades — that in spite of her divine nature and calling, she can be more or less perfectly conformed to Christ.

And if the Church is going to be renewed in a noticeable and fruitful way in our lifetimes, it's going to have to begin with recognizing, and committing to fulfilling, this call to perfection.

Light of the Nations

The Second Vatican Council's dogmatic constitution on the Church, *Lumen Gentium* ("Light of the Nations"), reflected beautifully on the Church's dual nature—anchored in heaven but bound to earth, united to Christ but a vessel of sinners:

> While Christ, holy, innocent and undefiled[8] knew nothing of sin,[9] but came to expiate only the sins of the people,[10] the Church, embracing in its bosom sinners, at the same time holy and always in need of being purified, always follows the way of penance and renewal. (8)

The early twentieth-century English writer Hilaire Belloc made a similar point in his own distinctive way:

> The Catholic Church is an institution I am bound to hold divine—but for unbelievers a proof of its divinity might be found in the fact that no merely human institution conducted with such knavish imbecility would have lasted a fortnight.[11]

---

[8] Heb. 7:26.
[9] 2 Cor. 5:21.
[10] Cf. Heb. 2:17.
[11] Robert Speaight, *The Life of Hilaire Belloc* (New York: Farrar, Straus and Cudahy, 1957), 383.

The Prodigal Church

Whether you prefer the formulation of the Council Fathers or the dyspeptic Englishman, the point is the same: The Church, in a remarkable mystery, contains within herself divinity *and* all the foibles and imperfections and evils that fallen human beings are capable of. The question, at any given time, is whether the human beings who comprise her are trying to embrace godliness or wallow in fallenness. This, just as it is for every person who claims to follow Christ, is "the way of penance and renewal."

In fact, *Lumen Gentium* speaks several times of Church renewal, and each time in terms of openness to the light and life of God:

- By the power of the Gospel He makes the Church keep the freshness of youth. Uninterruptedly He renews it and leads it to perfect union with its Spouse. (4)
- Moving forward through trial and tribulation, the Church is strengthened by the power of God's grace, which was promised to her by the Lord, so that in the weakness of the flesh she may not waver from perfect fidelity, but remain a bride worthy of her Lord, and moved by the Holy Spirit may never cease to renew herself, until through the Cross she arrives at the light which knows no setting. (9)
- It is not only through the sacraments and the ministries of the Church that the Holy Spirit sanctifies and leads the people of God and enriches it with virtues, but, "allotting his gifts to everyone according as He wills,"[12] He distributes special graces among the faithful of every rank. By these gifts He makes them fit and ready to undertake the various tasks and offices which contribute toward the renewal and building up of the Church. (12)

The Church renews herself and the world when she becomes, in a sense, transparent, allowing the grace of her Spouse both to

---

[12] 1 Cor. 12:11.

permeate her and to be transmitted to the people of God and all they encounter. She must, in another apparent paradox, maintain that spiritual transparency while also maintaining her timeless solidity in doctrine and in charity. The mystery, though, is alluring, attracting the people of the world to the impossibility, on purely human terms, of her existence. Her distinctiveness as an institution both reveals God and, precisely in doing so, draws us to Him.

You see, Jesus doesn't need a PR consultancy; He doesn't need a brand; He doesn't need focus groups. These worldly efforts only get in the way. When the Church embraces the methods of the world, whether in the bourgeois spirit described in the last chapter or in the bloodless "best practices" of a corporation or nongovernmental organization, her identity and its allure—that is, the Person of Jesus Christ—are obscured.

What Jesus can use are fearless prophets and radical signs of contradiction who, in their methods and their message, point the world to Him.

Faithful Shepherds

There aren't as many bishops among the canonized saints as you might think. Some of my very favorite saints were bishops in the early centuries of the Church—Ambrose and his protégé Augustine, Basil the Great, and Martin of Tours—but it's common in saintly bishop stories that the men don't seek out the honor. Ambrose and Martin, for instance, were selected by acclamation and merely acceded to the will of the people of God. What makes these saints so wonderful is how gracefully—literally full of grace—they handled their overwhelming responsibilities.

St. John Chrysostom, himself a bishop, is said to have quipped darkly, "The road to hell is paved with the bones of priests and monks, and the skulls of bishops are the lampposts that light the path." The quote is apocryphal, but the Church Father did have much to say about the episcopacy (as he did about everything else). To the extent he discussed the unlikelihood of the salvation of bishops, he emphasized the extraordinary pressures they are under—and the miniscule margins for error:

> Did you but know that a Bishop is bound to belong to all, to bear the burden of all; that others, if they are angry, are pardoned, but he never; that others, if they sin, have excuses made for them, he has none; you would not be eager for the dignity, would not run after it. So it is, the Bishop is exposed to the tongues of all, to the criticism of all, whether they be wise or fools. He is harassed with cares every day, nay, every night. He has many to hate him, many to envy him....
>
> To pass over every thing else: if one soul depart unbaptized, does not this subvert all his own prospect of salvation? The loss of one soul carries with it a penalty which no language can represent. For if the salvation of that soul was of such value, that the Son of God became man, and suffered so much, think how sore a punishment must the losing of it bring! And if in this present life he who is cause of another's destruction is worthy of death, much more in the next world. Do not tell me, that the presbyter is in fault, or the deacon. The guilt of all these comes perforce upon the head of those who ordained them.[13]

Every ambitious seminarian should be required to read the entire sermon, and perhaps commit it to memory. Beginning our discussion

[13] John Chrysostom, "Homily 3 on the Acts of the Apostles," trans. J. Walker, J. Sheppard, and H. Browne, rev. George B. Stevens, in *Nicene and Post-Nicene Fathers*, vol. 11, ed. Philip Schaff (Buffalo: Christian Literature Publishing Co., 1889), http://www.newadvent.org/fathers/210103.htm.

of the Church's hierarchy with this reminder of the otherworldly challenges it faces is meant to guide us away from the spluttering contempt that is increasingly common among the faithful. As one of my own parish priests reminded our congregation recently: The laity and even everyday priests are not responsible for, and will not be judged on, the administration of the Church. But we are responsible for our own souls and those under our care — including growing in the virtue of piety, by which we give due respect to our spiritual fathers. Let us (to quote Voltaire wildly out of context) tend our own gardens.

Bishops, in contrast, will be so judged. And while vengeance belongs to the Lord, we must say something about how they can better use the dignity and the authority of their offices to advance the cause of renewal.

It is the historical norm in the Church for the faithful not to have a terribly high opinion of their ecclesial authorities. And this has often been for good reason: Through the centuries these honors have attracted vain and often quite spectacularly corrupt men — and they obviously continue to do so today, and will continue to do so until Christ returns. Today we are seeing a reversion to that norm, with the laity's impression of hierarchical dithering and pusillanimity in response to crisis — whether sex abuse in the Church or the general degradation of our politics and culture — taking center stage.

What the Church needs from her bishops is the same thing she needs from all of us: holiness. Sometimes their genuine holiness will immediately satiate the demands of the faithful and the secular world, but much more often it will not. (You don't have to read far into the stories of sainted hierarchs to find that out.) But immediate, gratifying success isn't the point. Glorifying God is the point, and the fruits that holiness bears in this world might take longer to ripen than we'd prefer.

Living in prayerful simplicity is a good first step. Shedding episcopal mansions can be good — perhaps to charities rather than developers if possible — but it'll be quickly identified as a stunt if not accompanied by personal humility. Expertly crafted press releases announcing the sale undermine the credibility of the gesture, with the people and with the Lord. The same goes for acts of personal service, such as visiting prisons or washing the feet of the homeless on Holy Thursday: Sometimes the cameras can't be avoided, but if they can be, they should be. When things like this are perfectly packaged for YouTube by the diocesan social media squad, they look just like when professional athletes visit children's hospitals: heartwarming, but staged. Jesus' famous admonition applies to hierarchs just as surely as everybody else:

> Beware of practicing your piety before men in order to be seen by them; for then you will have no reward from your Father who is in heaven. Thus, when you give alms, sound no trumpet before you, as the hypocrites do in the synagogues and in the streets, that they may be praised by men. Truly, I say to you, they have their reward. But when you give alms, do not let your left hand know what your right hand is doing, so that your alms may be in secret; and your Father who sees in secret will reward you. (Matt. 6:1–4)

This doesn't mean that media-savvy prelates are all counterproductive and vainglorious. Surely some men are called to this kind of ministry. But bishops absolutely should not feel obligated to be stars.

In the same way that the Church shouldn't act like a corporation or an NGO, the bishops shouldn't seem like CEOs or executive directors. While I understand that Church institutions exist alongside civil legal regimes, chilly episcopal statements that clearly have been drafted by risk-minimizing attorneys should be avoided. It is right and good for dioceses to defend themselves strategically against unjust treatment, especially at the hands of unscrupulous governments and law firms that smell blood in the wake of scandal, but we should do so with quiet humility, remembering that while licitly defending the Church's material patrimony from being despoiled is virtuous, so is meekness. Sometimes giving up more than is strictly fair is what we need to do. Remember: *Penance* and renewal go together, and that penance may have to be borne by all of us, regardless of culpability. If everything we do is "sensible" in the eyes of the world, we're not being the signs of contradiction we're called to be.

Above all what we need from our bishops is boldness inspired by genuine personal holiness. This will mean, especially in those regions where the Church remains a significant public institution, being willing to give up some secular respectability for the sake of the Kingdom—for the sake of the authentic witness that draws souls to salvation. There is a real good in, for instance, maintaining a good relationship with the mayor's office, or with the leaders of the business community. But if that means not speaking out about a crackdown on pro-life pregnancy care centers or the exploitation of the poor through low wages and usury, then those relationships have become millstones.

Holy boldness may not—and, if it's authentic, almost certainly will not—satisfy all of our own expectations of our shepherds. But it's part of the bishop's calling to press forward, *to lead* amid the perpetual squabbling, as St. John Chrysostom described. And so let all of us pray for our bishops, and for the elevation of good men to the episcopacy, and for the grace to recognize genuine holiness when it might not be obvious.

Ambrosian Witness

Nobody likes the United States Conference of Catholic Bishops. Liberal Catholics say the conference acts as an arm of the

Republican Party and conservative Catholics say that the conference acts as an arm of the Democratic Party. Now, the fact of disagreement doesn't mean that neither side is right—I think even those who view the USCCB rather warmly would quibble with a few statements, or notable silences, here and there—but it does show that the bishops can't be easily pigeonholed, and that's a good thing.

But authentic public witness means more than annoying all sides equally, because that can just as easily come from broad-based timidity as from broad-based courage. As a general rule, I think we could stand to be a little louder, a little *more* political, while being very careful not to glom onto any faction or set of talking points. And I think history is on my side.

In the year 390, a mob in the provincial town of Thessalonica murdered an imperial official. St. Ambrose was then bishop of Milan, the Roman capital, and prevailed upon the Catholic emperor Theodosius I to respond peaceably. But the emperor then changed his mind, ordering an indiscriminate massacre of the people of the city. What happened next the old *Catholic Encyclopedia* called "one of most remarkable episodes in the history of the Church."[14]

Ambrose, known for his gentleness, wielded his spiritual authority against the emperor, refusing to say Mass in his presence until he repented. Anthony van Dyck's famous seventeenth-century portrayal of Ambrose's physically barring Theodosius from the Milan cathedral, one of my favorite paintings, probably isn't historically accurate: In humble prudence the bishop conducted this affair by private letter. But the emperor's penance was very public, including, St. Augustine related in his *City of God*, a public prostration

[14] James Loughlin, "St. Ambrose," in *The Catholic Encyclopedia*, vol. 1 (New York: Robert Appleton Company, 1907), http://www.newadvent.org/cathen/01383c.htm.

and confession in the cathedral. The historian Theodoret relates that, years later, Theodosius said, "I know no bishop worthy of the name, except Ambrose."

This wasn't about Ambrose's "winning"—though the assertion of ecclesial authority even over the emperor set a groundbreaking precedent. It was about Ambrose's fulfilling his duty with prudence but without fear. It was about a bishop's demonstration that nothing, not even his own standing (and thus the Church's standing) with the emperor, was worth the diabolical scandal of appearing to tolerate grave sin. It was about the Church's *being the Church*, holding the faithful to account for the good of their souls, and to give good example to the world.

Theodosius was a better man than today's Catholic politicians, the vast majority of whom would publicly sulk and rebuke, if not outright defy, such a correction from legitimate authority. But to what extent is that spiritual weakness among the faithful the result of generations of pusillanimous "tolerance" from the Church in the service of bourgeois respectability? I wonder what might have happened, at that time and ever since, if a bishop had rebuked President Kennedy for his public and private scandals. But that would have threatened the mainstream acceptance we had worked so long to achieve. Ambrose weeps.

The truth is that the Church can and must be political without being reliably partisan. Some see any engagement with the political as inherently corrupting; thus renewal only seems possible with a kind of undefiled detachment from public affairs. But this simply is not an option. First, politics is simply the organization of our common life, and thus is clearly within the Church's competence. (For the same reason, so is economics.) Second, there is no neutrality in politics, least of all for the Church. Silence as the poor are oppressed, the unborn killed, and ignorant souls damned will be judged harshly.

The Prodigal Church

A renewed, *Ambrosian* Church will cultivate detachment not from politics itself, but from political fear. We must understand that there can be no lasting rapprochement with the increasingly deranged, rapacious, even pagan American order. What does the Church have to lose for condemning usury, as we did for centuries, and sanctioning pickets of predatory payday lenders and denying Communion to profiteering bankers? Will donations from usurers dry up? I know Jesus taught in that challenging parable that we should "make friends for [ourselves] by means of unrighteous mammon" (Luke 16:9), but if securing that mammon means failing to correct the unrighteous and allowing them to damn themselves, then so will we be damned.

We could go on: What does the Church have to lose for absolutely condemning the failure to pay a just wage, as Pope Pius XI did in *Quadragesimo Anno* in 1931 — a teaching repeated but never really enforced by every pope since? Will CEOs stop ponying up for the bishop's appeal? Will certain politicians stop taking our calls? Will we get mocked by functionalistic, atheistic materialists for "not understanding economics," which apparently requires that some people just have to starve so others can own yachts? As Christ said, "For what will it profit a man, if he gains the whole world and forfeits his life?" (Matt. 16:26).

I used two economic examples, but it's that same fear of ostracism, financial and political and social, that keeps some prelates quiet on essential topics like marriage and abortion. Faintheartedness in the "culture war" is not distinct from but absolutely connected to faintheartedness in condemning other social and economic injustices. It's a habit that becomes a moral contagion in the Church, blunting our witness to the truth of Christ. The question is this: Which injustices are we willing to fight, even with the worldly costs of doing so? The answer should be all of them.

A renewed Church is a *consistent* Church. This is the seamless garment—the *real thing*, not the *brand*.

A New Seamless Garment

The phrase "seamless garment" was popularized by Cardinal Joseph Bernardin in the 1980s to describe what has come to be known as a "consistent ethic of life" approach to politics, which insists on the inherent relationship between abortion and other issues, such as economic justice and militarism. Articulated in this limited way, it clearly describes reality. It has become, however, a buzz phrase used by many specifically to *deemphasize* abortion more than actually to *elevate* other issues, and so it has been delegitimized.

And this is a real shame, because the concept, as well as the image it comes from, is beautiful and haunting: "When the soldiers had crucified Jesus they took his garments and made four parts, one for each soldier; also his tunic. But the tunic was without seam, woven from top to bottom" (John 19:23). The truth of Christ, whether in abstract theological dogma or in genuine social justice or in the life of holiness, is held together in unbroken perfection. It has an eternal integrity.

We've talked about this with regard to political witness, but the Church has suffered from disintegration—and can be renewed with a commitment to integrity—in other ways as well. Chief among these are the everyday disciplines that used to give order and distinctiveness to Catholic living. If our lives look just like everyone else's, how can our witness to the transforming power of Christ's grace be credible?

I'm familiar with a gala held several years ago by a Catholic social services agency. It was the big event of the year for the organization and one of the more established functions on its city's social calendar—the kind of event where the local paper does fawning write-ups of who was seen wearing what. (We're already getting into dangerous territory.) They had valet parking and an open bar and delicate hors d'oeuvres passed by tuxedoed servers—you get the idea.

It was also a Friday, and the plated dinner was entirely meaty —no vegetarian or pescatarian options. Of course, the law of the Church mandating Friday abstinence from meat was loosened by the American bishops in the wake of Vatican II; now abstinence can be replaced with some other penitential practice. But Fridays are still penitential days and abstinence still the standard prescribed penance. You would never have known that at the gala, though: Everyone, including the local bishop, partied the night away as if it were any other day of the week.

Every Friday is meant to be a small Good Friday, a day of penance in remembrance of Christ's suffering and death. While specific traditions have shifted over the centuries, honoring these days has been part of being a Christian since the earliest days of the Church. But when Church institutions blatantly ignore this tradition, how can we expect the average layperson to understand it or to take it seriously? The point of Friday penance is to remember and to participate in some small way in Christ's Passion. If the institutional Church can't be bothered to spare a thought for Christ Crucified once a week, should we be surprised when lay Catholics organize their lives around parties and football games instead of Masses and the liturgical calendar?

It's contemptuous of the Church's tradition and of her Spouse to schedule Church-affiliated bashes on Fridays. If, for some reason, it's absolutely impossible not to, then some kind of recognition of the solemn day—salmon or lobster aren't even that penitential!—should be made. But let's be honest: It's never *really* necessary to have a blowout on a penitential day. If research says that contributions are maximized on Fridays, then shred the research, schedule the event for a different day, and trust God to make up the difference. He's not bound by the latest in fundraising science.

Not only is running roughshod over spiritual disciplines bad for the soul; it's bad for our witness. From the very beginning it's been little idiosyncrasies — the Sign of the Cross, holy water, other sacramentals — that have built up Catholic identity and shown the world that we're different. Of course all of these little habits have to be married to a real transformation of soul, but that transformative grace is signaled and, through acts of prayer and kindness and personal service, transmitted to others by our willingness to *live differently*.

A generous non-Catholic donor who witnessed that gala would come away seeing the agency as just another in the constellation of regional charitable organizations. While the nice videos about the agency's work showed that its workers and volunteers were compassionate and effective, so are the teams of most other organizations. Setting aside the disproportionate number of Roman collars in the room, the whole thing could just as well have been a United Way or Salvation Army benefit dinner. That's a dissipated Church.

The Little Things

A renewed Church is one that's confident in her identity in Christ and in Christian tradition, *especially* when what that calls for is strange or incomprehensible to the secular world. The Church, in her institutions and as the Body of Christ, is meant to manifest Him to all the nations; we cannot succeed in this if we are in every visible way indistinguishable from the crowd.

We've already talked about Friday abstinence. To this day, even as Catholics have largely abandoned the practice, restaurants in regions influenced by Catholic culture have seafood specials on Fridays out of habit. It's a testament to the endurance of cultural habits, even as the spiritual motivation behind them has faded. A renewed emphasis on this tradition from our spiritual fathers would not only revive a distinctive cultural practice, but restore the liturgical mini-drama that unfolds every week.

On a personal note: Adopting a weekly Friday penance, followed by light but intentional indulgence on Sundays (little Easters), has helped me to recognize and to embrace the spiritual realities that are hiding in plain sight. The seven-day week is not arbitrary; it was branded onto the human soul at the creation of the universe. Living each week with intentionality, culminating in a little Triduum, has been one of the most fruitful spiritual practices I have adopted. And its benefits would be compounded in community with others.

Speaking of which: Reconsecrating Sundays should be emphasized by every pastor and bishop in the country. This is a lot harder than giving up meat on Fridays because it requires the complete overhaul of family habits—something we're still working on in my home—but the fruits are worth it. Until very recently the Church *strictly* forbade unnecessary servile work and commercial activity on the Sabbath in accord with the Third Commandment. This included, in particular, admonishing employers not to require workers to labor on this day. And the thing is that these prohibitions haven't changed! But as the world has deemphasized the Sabbath, so has the Church.

The fact is that we no longer live in a sabbatical culture—a culture where rest is valued and genuine leisure protected. The repeal of Sunday commerce prohibitions, the so-called blue laws, will be remembered as one of the most important milestones in secularization. It's a scandal how quickly the Church acquiesced to treating Sunday as nothing more than Mass day—and in doing so she contributed to the decline of Mass-going, as well. A recent economics paper demonstrated a clear link between the repeal of blue laws and decreased church attendance: When there are more options for business or entertainment on the table, Jesus Christ starts to look less appealing.

Reducing Sundays to Mass days has also meant accepting the dominant, secular, private approach to religious practice. The Sabbath is meant to be, and was through nearly all of the Church's history, consecrated to Christ *in its entirety*. The sequestration of this consecration to the one hour (give or take) we spend in the church building is an act of secular aggression against the rightful dominion of Christ the King, and the Church has abandoned the field of battle. Even if we can no longer convince the civil authorities to enact laws honoring the Sabbath in its fullness, we can remind the faithful to do so by our habits.

As the visible Church, we can and must direct the world to Christ in visible ways. If we appear to be (or, in fact, are) embarrassed of Him, then, quite simply, we will fail. And that would betray the rest of the Church: the perfect communion of saints and angels from whom we receive confidence and succor, and to whom we owe our very best efforts to extend the Kingdom of God on earth.

4

The Invisible Church

The Forgotten

We live in an age of suspicion and cynicism toward established institutions. The U.S. Congress's approval rating hovers in the teens and twenties—and has for several years now, with no springtime of public confidence in sight. Elite-skeptical politicians and social movements rise among the people precisely in response to the discomfort they generate among the establishment. The only institutions in American life that are consistently rated trustworthy are the ones with the guns: law enforcement and the military, though the former is losing ground.

It goes without saying that the Church has not been insulated from the anti-establishment firestorm, and that in her own misdeeds she has stoked it. It is in vogue now, even and especially among Catholics, to speak of the institutional Church in the same way a civil libertarian speaks of the federal government: at best a necessary evil, a leviathan than needs to be reined in, even a threat to genuine faith and conscience.

I get it. We just spent an entire chapter discussing how the Church, by renewing her confident self-understanding as Christ's Bride, Body, and earthly mediator, can and will be renewed by His grace. But that can all feel abstract and a bit naïve alongside the accumulation of scandal and dithering and moral weakness. Sure, we might have faith that God *can* accomplish the renewal of the earthly Church, but dare we hope that it's possible, on the horizon of the coming years and decades, or even generations and centuries? It can seem far-fetched.

This defeatism, though, misses a huge part of what the Church *is*, right now. Dioceses and curial congregations, chanceries and secretariats, schools and hospitals and charities: These are all part of the visible Church that we interact with every day. But there's also the Church in heaven, which is just as real — in fact, based on the theory of being we discussed last chapter, *more real* for her direct and perpetual participation in God's life — as anything we see here on earth. Here's how *Lumen Gentium* describes this awe-some relationship:

> For all who are in Christ, having His Spirit, form one Church and cleave together in Him.[15] Therefore the union of the wayfarers with the brethren who have gone to sleep in the peace of Christ is not in the least weakened or interrupted, but on the contrary, according to the perpetual faith of the Church, is strengthened by communication of spiritual goods. For by reason of the fact that those in heaven are more closely united with Christ, they establish the whole Church more firmly in holiness, lend nobility to the worship which the Church offers to God here on earth and in many ways contribute to its greater edification.[16] For after they have been received into their heavenly home and are present to the Lord,[17] through Him and with Him and in Him they do not cease to intercede with the Father for us,

[15] Cf. Eph. 4:16.
[16] Cf. 1 Cor. 12:12–27.
[17] Cf. 2 Cor. 5:8.

showing forth the merits which they won on earth through the one Mediator between God and man,[18] serving God in all things and filling up in their flesh those things which are lacking of the sufferings of Christ for His Body which is the Church. (49)

In the Creed at every Mass we profess faith in "the communion of saints," which refers specifically to the "cloud of witnesses" (Heb. 12:1) who continually regard us and God from their eternal rest. But this image can feel distant and abstracted, as if we're toughing it out in the stadium while getting cheered on by white-robed spectators. What the Vatican II Fathers are telling us, though, in continuity with the teaching of the Church through the ages, is that we have a *more* intimate relationship with the saints than we do even with our fellow "wayfarers." Through "the communication of spiritual goods"—that is, the prayers we offer through them and the graces they mediate to us—we benefit directly from their unity with the Lord, while among the earthbound we can only share reflections of that divine life.

Thus the Church's relationship with Christ is dependent not just on the holiness of her earthly members and leaders, but on the real, ongoing, unbreakable bond between the Church Triumphant—the saints and angels—and the trinitarian God. This is why we can say, again in the ritual of the Creed, that the Church is genuinely "holy"—not potentially but really, right now, as we speak, and for all time. The invisible Church is our celestial anchor of holiness, the perfection to which we are called that is not a theoretical future possibility, but an ongoing present reality.

There is no better cure for ecclesial despair than remembering, honoring, and relating to this cloud of witnesses.

---

[18] Cf. 1 Tim. 2:5.

The Prodigal Church

Dirty Hands

In its consideration of the Church's relationship with the saints, *Lumen Gentium* begins by describing the example they offer to us:

> When we look at the lives of those who have faithfully followed Christ, we are inspired with a new reason for seeking the City that is to come[19] and at the same time we are shown a most safe path by which among the vicissitudes of this world, in keeping with the state in life and condition proper to each of us, we will be able to arrive at perfect union with Christ, that is, perfect holiness. In the lives of those who, sharing in our humanity, are however more perfectly transformed into the image of Christ,[20] God vividly manifests His presence and His face to men. He speaks to us in them, and gives us a sign of His Kingdom, to which we are strongly drawn, having so great a cloud of witnesses over us and such a witness to the truth of the Gospel. (50)

The Council Fathers were laser-focused on the way the saints imitate Christ and thus invite us to closer and, ultimately, perfect union with Him. I'm particularly struck by the claim that the saints offer "a most safe path" to Christ. While it's always possible that we, and the Church as an institution and as the people of God, might discover some truly innovative path to holiness, more likely than not we will follow in the footsteps of the spiritual masters through the ages. One of the most important lessons that we should draw from saintly examples is that holiness is rarely practical or respectable in worldly terms.

In contrast, there's a kind of "dirty hands" pragmatism that has seeped into the way we think about our institutions, civil and

---

[19] Cf. Heb. 13:14; 11:10.
[20] Cf. 2 Cor. 3:18.

ecclesial. The idea is that the only way to survive in a fallen and dangerous world is for some hard-nosed people to "get their hands dirty" by making otherwise immoral decisions that preserve the life and liberty of the greater population. The classic example is torture: Some Christian theorists[21], especially in the chaotic days after September 11, genuinely argued that while torture was wrong always and everywhere, sometimes it was *required* because the consequences of *not torturing* (in, say, a ticking time bomb scenario) would be worse. The thesis throws the very idea of morality into incoherence.

There is an analogue in the life of the Church. True holiness is sometimes thought to be reserved for those who can safely practice it—monks and nuns and quiet families—who basically freeload on the hard work of hierarchs and lawyers and executives and so on, all of whom see to the business of maintaining the institutions that make quiet holiness possible. In this way of thinking, lay and clerical leaders have to "get their hands dirty" by making compromises with their consciences to sustain the institutions. Needless to say, this is how you end up with cover-up cabals: In attempting to preserve the institution's standing at the cost of its soul, we lose everything.

More prosaically, we see this kind of thinking when Catholic figures, including bishops and other Church officials, put on a secular face in the public square, offering generic words in response to news events or censoring the name of Christ to avoid giving "offense" or appearing "sectarian." To be seen as *too Catholic* would risk losing public privileges and esteem, even being seen as unserious or foolish. The intent, at its most sincere, is to preserve the public influence of the Church; the result, invariably, is to signal to the

---

[21] See Jean Bethke Elshtain, "Reflection on the Problem of 'Dirty Hands'" in *Torture: A Collection*, ed. Sanford Levinson (Oxford, UK: Oxford University Press, 2004), 77–93.

faithful that we should accept the strict privatization of our Faith, and that we should be embarrassed of Christ.

The saints demonstrate for us a higher practicality, one that not only rejects but radically undermines our culture's prevailing materialism: holiness at all costs. St. Paul wrote to the Corinthians,

> For I think that God has exhibited us apostles as last of all, like men sentenced to death; because we have become a spectacle to the world, to angels and to men. We are fools for Christ's sake.... When reviled, we bless; when persecuted, we endure; when slandered, we try to conciliate; we have become, and are now, as the refuse of the world, the offscouring of all things. (1 Cor. 4:9–10, 12–13)

This doesn't mean we have to reject all cleverness: St. Thomas More tried every legal and rhetorical maneuver he could imagine to save himself from Henry VIII's wrath, but he preserved his well-formed conscience all along, and accepted death when no licit options remained. But even as he tried to employ the practices of the world—the civil law—to preserve himself, above all he wielded the practices of heaven in his devotion to prayer and mortification.

I don't think it's a coincidence that, in a time and culture organized around self-interest, the Spirit has raised up holy men and women whose distinguishing virtues are meekness and simplicity. At around the same time, both the United States and Canada were blessed with such examples—both men unimpressive in health, strength, and education; both assigned as porters (doormen or receptionists) by their orders; and both hailed by their cities for their heavenly radiance and miracle-working: Bl. Solanus Casey of Detroit (1870–1957) and St. Andre Bessette of Montreal (1845–1937).

I have a special devotion to St. Andre because it was at St. Joseph's Oratory in Montreal, built to honor his patron saint and to recognize the notoriety St. Andre's miracles had brought to the

Holy Cross Fathers, that I first felt the stirrings that culminated in my return to the sacraments. It was simplicity and humility that drew me: his own, and that of the pilgrims who still visit him. When I saw a child in a wheelchair touch Andre's onyx tomb and bow his head, it felt like the first time I'd witnessed genuine, faithful, hopeful, desperate prayer. I don't know if he was healed, but I was.

Bl. Solanus should be America's patron for the twenty-first century. The sixth of sixteen siblings, his voice was damaged by diphtheria as a child and his education never advanced beyond high school. He followed the promptings of God, though, and entered the Capuchin order in Detroit. Due to his limitations he was ordained a "simplex" priest, able to say Mass but unable to preach or to hear confessions. Yet, like Andre up north, he became known around the city not through press releases or media blitzes, but his own simple holiness.

He is the antithesis of every archetype of American success—the ambitious pioneer, the credentialed meritocrat, the savvy entrepreneur. And yet we should—we must—resist with every bit of our spirit the idea that Bl. Solanus was "impractical." He went where God told him, not where he desired to go; he accumulated heavenly honors, not worldly ones; he built nothing that made money or collected rent, but he built up his soul and those around him. In so doing—and in his continuing heavenly ministry—he has done more good than every Silicon Valley billionaire combined. Pretending that God doesn't exist, that prayers aren't efficacious, and that grace doesn't elevate our world isn't practical at all: The godless, saint-less, angel-less world is the fantasy, and when Christians act as though it's reality out of a misplaced pragmatism, we give in to despair.

It's the dirty hands of the simple and the humble, not of the wealthy and the powerful, that have always built up God's Church in holiness. Renewal begins with anchoring our hopes in *their* example and intercession, not the ministry of money and influence.

The Prodigal Church

Living with the Saints

It's true that human dignity is inalienable. That means that there's nothing that can happen to us, nor any stage of life we will go through, that will extinguish the image of God within us. The unborn and the elderly, the terminally sick and the profoundly disabled, the depressed and the lonely: All of these people are increasingly marginalized in our culture, told implicitly or explicitly that they are burdensome, valueless, unworthy, or broken beyond repair. This is the necessary trajectory of a secular, materialist culture, and it's a demonic denial of God's goodness and love.

But our dignity is not invulnerable. As with any of the human qualities that we get from and share with God, we can act *with* or *against* it. When we act against our conscience and our reason, for instance, we weaken them for the next time we need them. In so doing, we assault the image of God within us, damaging our dignity.

We can, of course, never *annihilate* that dignity any more than we can *annihilate* our nature itself. But we can chip away at it, thus making it less apparent to others—and to ourselves. Over time, as we frustrate the work of grace within us and become accustomed to our disfigurement, we can forget what that image of God, that dignity, looks like and demands from us. When we try to go our own way and follow the logic of the world, just as when the institutional Church does the same, it can become harder and harder to remember what we are called to be.

But there is always healing. This, too, is part of our dignity—that through the grace that comes from relationship with the Lord, it can be restored, and ultimately enhanced to its fullest perfection. Dignity belongs first to God, and when we live with dignity we reflect Him to others. And we, as individuals and as the Church, can approach the fullness of human dignity by recognizing that it already exists within the Church in the form of the saints.

For just as Christian communion among wayfarers brings us closer to Christ, so our companionship with the saints joins us to Christ, from Whom as from its Fountain and Head issues every grace and the very life of the people of God. It is supremely fitting, therefore, that we love those friends and coheirs of Jesus Christ, who are also our brothers and extraordinary benefactors, that we render due thanks to God for them and "suppliantly invoke them and have recourse to their prayers, their power and help in obtaining benefits from God through His Son, Jesus Christ, who is our Redeemer and Saviour."[22] For every genuine testimony of love shown by us to those in heaven, by its very nature tends toward and terminates in Christ who is the "crown of all saints,"[23] and through Him, in God Who is wonderful in his saints and is magnified in them. (LG 50)

Notice the different verbs used in that first sentence: Earthbound relationships among Christians "bring us closer to Christ," while prayerful communion with the saints "joins us" to Him. The saints offer us privileged access to the Lord, which we can enjoy *right now* due to our shared membership in His Body, the Church. We not only imitate the dignity of the saints, but through their intercession, our dignity can be enhanced.

This awesome truth is so often obscured because the institutional Church fails to act with saintly dignity. We mustn't expect immediate perfection, or else we will always be frustrated. But the Church can be more or less transparent to the heavenly reality, and make it more or less clear to the faithful and the rest of the world that the saints are real and accessible and alive — more alive than

---

[22] Council of Trent, Session XXV, "On the Invocation, Veneration, and Relics, of Saints, and on Sacred Images."

[23] Roman Breviary, Invitatory for the Feast of All Saints.

we are. A renewed Church will be one that celebrates the saints, yes, but also one that is unashamed about appealing to them and living with their radical *holiness at all costs.*

The trick the devil plays is to convince us that no one will understand, that whatever good might be done will be overwhelmed by the sneering and the mockery. Sometimes it's pride that causes us to value our reputation too highly, but sometimes it's that misplaced pragmatism by which we rationalize that losing face means losing souls. But the Romans laughed at us (and much worse than that) and we ended up co-opting their empire and culture to bring Christ to all the corners of the earth.

It's the same now as then: *It's precisely because no one will understand* that we should lean into mysterious (but authentic) devotions and public appeals to the Church Triumphant. It's precisely the weirdness—and our meek but steadfast response to the mockery it will generate—that will attract people who are disoriented by postmodernism and consumerism and radical skepticism.

Christ was willing to alienate every last one of His followers by delivering the hardest and strangest parts of His message with clarity. Are we?

Bridge to Heaven

When we think about the most challenging Christian teachings in twenty-first-century America, sexual morality is the first thing to come to mind. To some degree it has always been this way: Christ's teaching on divorce earned Him a mild rebuke from His disciples (Matt. 19:10), and many of the early martyrs were killed for refusing to surrender their bodies to the desires of brutish pagans. The Christian concept of the fully incarnated God, the Word made flesh, gives us a highly elevated view of the human body, which comes with spectacular dignity—and the laws that govern and respect it.

But it was a different incarnate reality that chased away Christ's followers, and that remains His most vexing teaching of all: the Eucharist.

I don't mean to suggest that Church renewal depends on *deemphasizing* sexual morality—far from it. It was precisely the dignity that early Christian sexual teachings and practices accorded to women that drew so many women to the Church, often along with members of their families and households. The Church should not compromise one bit, *especially* as the bitter fruits of the sexual revolution are becoming increasingly obvious even to those who participate in the culture it spawned. It would be tragic indeed if the Church acquiesced to the new bourgeois[24] just as it fell into disrepute, and just as her steadfastness might be rewarded.

Rather, I mean that the Church must strongly emphasize the Eucharist and the Holy Sacrifice of the Mass at which the heavens open and Christ becomes fully present to us. This is where the Church's complex reality as both earthly *and* heavenly, *and* as the bridge between the two, is made fully manifest. This is where we convince the curious of the indispensability of the Church: Teachings on sexuality and related social issues get you part of the way there, but they are shared by other traditions, while the Eucharist belongs to Jesus Christ alone.

Until very recently I didn't have a favorite chapter or verse of Scripture. Honestly, I didn't know Scripture well enough to have any opinions about it at all, except a vague notion that the

---

[24] It should go without saying that we must defend the Church's sexual teachings, just as with everything else, not on the basis that they are *respectable* but on the basis that they are *radical*. It's not the 1950s anymore, and even in the 1950s, the seeds of the 1960s were being sown. Cohabitation, divorce, contraception, and even abortion are now fully ensconced in bourgeois morality: They are all considered not just *respectable* but *responsible* choices.

Old Testament was often tedious. But in my work as an editor of Catholic books, and increasingly in my everyday life, I've been blessed to encounter Scripture more and more. And now I can say with confidence that my favorite chapter is John 6: the Bread of Life discourse, where Christ instructs His followers to eat His flesh and drink His blood. And my favorite verse is the answer to every doubt. It was given by Peter after the throngs, in confusion and dismay, left Christ: "Lord, to whom shall we go? You have the words of eternal life" (John 6:68).

Wouldn't it be great if we acted with confidence in that truth? If we didn't worry about worldly respectability or prestige, "measurable outcomes" or "implementation schemes," but about simply offering "the words of eternal life"? Christ may have announced the founding of the Church when He told Peter, "On this rock I will build my church" (Matt. 16:18), and He may have announced her mission when He told His apostles to "make disciples of all nations, baptizing them in the name of the Father and of the Son and of the Holy Spirit, teaching them to observe all that I have commanded you" (Matt. 28:19–20). But I like to think that it was with Peter's simple expression of loyalty that the Church's *self-understanding*, when she is at her very best, was articulated: She brings to the world what no one else can, the words of eternal life.

And so, as we will discuss in greater detail in the next section, the Mass is the focal point of renewal. It is where the Church's heavenly reality and earthly purpose collide, resulting in an unfathomable release of spiritual energy—of grace. Yes, those famous words of *Lumen Gentium* are true: The Eucharist is the "source and summit of the whole Christian life."[25] But it is also much more: It—*He*—is

---

[25] LG no. 11. The phrase is also translated as "fount and apex," but that's not as quotable.

the source and summit of the life of every person and family and community and nation on the earth. The Mass is for *everyone*.

This is true, of course, because Christ is for everyone: The grace of the Mass is the spiritual energy that powers the engine of genuine human progress. Every person who participates in the Mass benefits in a special way from this grace, but so does the whole world—in part due to the prayers and good works of those congregants. We can see this universality—this catholicity—in the words and reality of the Mass itself. This is no clearer than in the Sanctus, the thrice-holy prayer of the angels recorded by the prophet Isaiah:

> I saw the Lord sitting upon a throne, high and lifted up; and his train filled the temple. Above him stood the seraphim; each had six wings: with two he covered his face, and with two he covered his feet, and with two he flew. And one called to another and said: "Holy, holy, holy is the LORD of hosts; the whole earth is full of his glory." And the foundations of the thresholds shook at the voice of him who called, and the house was filled with smoke. (Isa. 6:1–4)

I have an old missal from the 1940s with a full-page engraving of the altar accompanying this prayer. The crucified Christ, the Holy Spirit, and God the Father are all present, but perhaps most striking and haunting are the saints and angels in the background, assisting in the sacrifice and adoring it. Their presence isn't some outdated or esoteric teaching. The priest proclaims it immediately before the Consecration in the Preface of the Eucharistic Prayer:

> And so, with Angels and Archangels, with Thrones and Dominions, and with all the hosts and Powers of heaven, we sing the hymn of your glory.

St. John Chrysostom says it as clearly as possible: "The angels surround the priest. The whole sanctuary and the space before the altar is filled with the heavenly Powers come to honor Him who is present upon the altar."[26] And throughout the ages holy men and women have been granted visions of this tremendous reality. St. Bridget of Sweden wrote in her startling *Revelations*:

> One day, when I was assisting at the Holy Sacrifice, I saw an immense number of holy angels descend and gather around the altar, contemplating the priest. They sang heavenly canticles that ravished my heart; heaven itself seemed to be contemplating the great Sacrifice.[27]

Three centuries earlier, the equally sublime St. Hildegard of Bingen recorded this vision:

> Hence when a priest clad in sacred vestments approached that altar to celebrate the divine mysteries, I saw that a great calm light was brought to it from Heaven by angels and shone around the altar until the sacred rite was ended and the priest had withdrawn from it. And when the Gospel of peace had been recited and the offering to be consecrated had been placed upon the altar, and the priest sang the praise of Almighty God, "Holy, Holy, Holy, Lord God of Hosts," which began the mystery of the sacred rites, Heaven was suddenly opened and a fiery and inestimable brilliance descended over that offering and irradiated it completely with light, as the sun illumines anything its rays shine through. And, thus illuminating it, the brilliance bore it on high into the secret places of Heaven and then replaced it on the altar, as a person draws in a breath and lets it out again; and thus

---

[26] *Treaty on the Priesthood*, Bk. 6, Para. 4.
[27] Bk. VIII.

the offering was made true flesh and true blood, although in human sight it looked like bread and wine.[28]

In the Mass, then, we participate in a real way in the perfect and perpetual worship of the angels and saints. There is not, and can never be, anything more important to human civilization than this. And we have it: The Church is its guardian, and it's ours to share, just as Jesus commanded us. What are we waiting for? With the angels and saints not only watching over us but present among us, what can we possibly fear?

The Gates of Hell

Renewal can begin only when the Church — in her institutions, her leaders, and the lay faithful — takes to heart her own glorious reality. The angels and saints are more fully members of the Church than we are; they want nothing more than to share their perfect love with their exiled confreres, and to make the earthbound Church more perfect in the process. Accepting this spiritual support by uniting our wills to the Lord's can do more to revitalize the Church and to extend God's Kingdom than a million consultant-designed strategies and flowcharts and PowerPoints can. The logic of the world has its place, but the Church has a higher calling and a higher dignity.

As each person must live up to his heavenly dignity, so must the Church live up to hers. It's an awesome responsibility, completely impossible for fallen creatures to fulfill on our own. But we have God's grace, and we have His promise:

And I say to thee: That thou art Peter; and upon this rock I will build my church, and the gates of hell shall not prevail

---

[28] Hildegard of Bingen, *Scivias*, Vision Six. http://www.columbia.edu/itc/english/f2003/client_edit/documents/scivias.html.

against it. And I will give to thee the keys of the kingdom of heaven. And whatsoever thou shalt bind upon earth, it shall be bound also in heaven: and whatsoever thou shalt loose upon earth, it shall be loosed also in heaven. (Matt. 16:18–19, Douay-Rheims)

The gates of hell can never prevail, but they can gain ground precisely when we lose sight of this fact—when we think the Church needs something other than Jesus Christ to thrive, when we think the Church needs the world instead of the other way around.

There's a lot of hand-wringing, especially on social media, about "saving the Church," either from secularists or leftists or traditionalists or anyone else we don't like. But the Church is already saved; she is the very instrument of the salvation of mankind. She doesn't just benefit from the "spiritual goods" communicated by the saints; she *includes* the saints and *is* the means by which they communicate God's divine life to us. She has, and can never lose, everything she needs.

And so what the Church doesn't need are people, lay or clerical, busying themselves with trying to "save" her. The result will always be self-aggrandizing attempts to apply the logic of the world to the Church's heavenly nature and dignity. What she does need are people, lay and clerical, committed first to their own dignity, their own holiness, their own love of God and neighbor. And the beautiful thing about genuine holiness is that it is *always* other-regarding, spreading grace to others to enhance their relationship with the Lord.

If we aim first for some worldly concept of "renewal," we'll lose sight of the real prize and never achieve it. If we aim first for God, we will, through the ministry of the angels and saints, allow Him to renew the Church.

Part 3

The Parish

5

Center of Life

The Third Place

We love living in a neighborhood with several places for just hanging out. The coffee shop is my go-to place for casual meetings, and a few of my friends in the neighborhood use it as an office when they work from home. There's a branch of the city library system with a kids' play area where parents can arrange simple playdates with friends. There are more than a few bars for drinks and darts and pool. And, when the weather is nice, families have two parks, each with a playground and fields and more, where kids can burn off energy and parents can, if only for a blessed moment, sit.

The other day I finally tested out another neighborhood hangout: Sal's Barber Shop, a nearly century-old institution in south Pittsburgh. The walls were lined with vintage barbering equipment, including several dozen old personalized shaving mugs and brushes. At least one man in the shop with me wasn't getting his hair cut at all: He was just there for the chitchat. A city police officer walked in just to visit with, I solemnly swear, his haul from the donut shop next door.

Judging by the photos on the walls, the original Sal (the current Sal's father) was partial to local Democratic politicians (the only kind of politician in Pittsburgh) and national Republicans; the elder

The Prodigal Church

Sal posed with Ronald Reagan and, on multiple occasions, long before he was a candidate for anything but an Emmy, Donald Trump. There was actually a disagreement among those present about the impeachment of President Trump but, in a glorious reminder of the possibility of decency, the dispute was aired in good humor.

Sociologists call these community assets "third places," where the "first place" is the home and the "second place" the workplace. Third places provide a neutral space for community members to meet and socialize; a buffer between domestic life and the dominion of the marketplace, bringing us out of our shells into a community defined by cooperation rather than competition. They are, at their best, places of good cheer that break down political and socioeconomic and cultural barriers—places where real community can be formed and the common good made manifest.

The decline of third places has been observed by social scientists and cultural critics for at least a generation now. At the same time, the first place has also receded as family life has become increasingly fragmented. Widespread divorce rends both households and intergenerational bonds, and young people are delaying marriage, often in perpetuity, preferring to live alone or in temporary cohabitation. The second place has taken the initiative against its competitors (market ideology can conceive of human relationships only in terms of zero-sum competition) and filled the vacuum: Our prevailing ethic of work emphasizes rivalry and efficiency and profit, and it has colonized not just our time but our space.

I'll let the geographers and demographers figure out the chain of causation, but this much is clear: The expansion of the second place at the expense of the first and third has coincided with a radical shift in the structure of our communities. Suburbanization destroyed the closeness of the three places, fencing off the home on a cul-de-sac and isolating the office on the other side of a lengthy commute. The third place—the in-between place—was lost in the shuffle. Social interactions now had to be well planned to accommodate car travel; serendipity, one of the hallmarks of a welcoming third place, was lost.

All of this has also coincided with the decline of the parish, perhaps the third place *par excellence*, as the center of Catholic life. No, we can't re-create the old Catholic "ghettos," where hundreds of families, often from the same town or region in the Old World, squeezed into teeming urban neighborhoods. Suburbanization is, if not irreversible, at the very least out of our control at this point. And the urban enclave model is fragile, as was demonstrated in the 1950s when, once respectability and prosperity were achieved, everyone fled to the land of the white picket fence.

But we can regard with genuine admiration and apply to our circumstances what was good about those communities. The parish as the center of life for the local people of God is the ideal. My mother grew up in a typically dense and hilly neighborhood in south Pittsburgh; she walked to Mass and Catholic school throughout her childhood; her first job was in the parish office; and the parish gymnasium was the center of neighborhood social life, whether for dances or fish fries or other events. Even if we can't recreate this, we can be inspired by it to create parishes where people *want to be*, even beyond their weekly liturgical duty.

My relatively third-place-rich neighborhood has a Catholic parish—three, in fact, as of this writing. (Two will be shuttered soon as part of the reorganization of our diocese.) The one closest to us had, at one point, the most parishioners and the most students in all of western Pennsylvania. It's not much of a third place now: The church is locked except for a few Masses a week—though weekly adoration is offered—and the boiler in the old school building is busted. Some parishioners graciously organized a Bible study with childcare for the young families in the neighborhood. It's a small but lovely reflection of what the place used to be.

The Prodigal Church

As we described in the last chapter, and will consider more fully in the next, the Mass is the most important human action imaginable — precisely because it isn't just a human activity, but a participation in heavenly life. And so we mustn't pooh-pooh a few Masses a week: The angels are just as present there as in more-thriving parishes. But one of the duties of the parish is to *extend* the grace of the sacraments to the surrounding community. This is where, as social and ecclesial trends work against us, we have to think boldly and creatively about *what it means to be a parish*, and how to manifest that in our day.

A Note on Diversity

Before we go on, we should pause briefly to discuss the diversity of experiences of Catholic life in America. My experience is in Pittsburgh, a typical Rust Belt town with a historic density of working-class Catholic immigrants. The population of Pittsburgh proper has declined more than fifty percent since World War II, and the Catholic population has dropped even more. The Church's infrastructure in this city was massively overbuilt, and we've been unwinding that excess for decades.

The story is more or less the same in a swath of America from the Midwest through New England: traditionally Catholic towns and cities with enormous investments in church buildings and institutions whose Catholic populations have cratered. But the story is not at all the same in places like San Antonio or Phoenix or even Atlanta, where parishes are teeming with domestic trans-plants and Latino immigrants, and where our infrastructure may be, if anything, underbuilt for the moment.

But if we look at the status quo as permanent, even as signs of trouble mount, we make the same mistake that Church leaders in places like Pittsburgh did a few generations ago. Texan suburban parishes, just like the Rust Belt ethnic enclaves of time gone by, will only be teeming two or three decades from now if the Church can retain the children of the newcomers—and the evidence is that we are not. The children of immigrants practice the Faith into adulthood at just about the same paltry rate as children of native-born American Catholics. They're assimilating to American norms, and that's not a good thing at all.

Therefore, while the situation *right now* in the American Church is very different from region to region, that's not going to last. Mexican and Central American immigration, whatever we might think about federal policy, can't last forever. And even if it does last for several more decades, it's only masking an institutional failure to retain the next generation—a crisis just as bad in New Mexico as in Connecticut.

While the examples I give and the portrait I sketch will often be distinctly Yankee Catholic, the problems—and the necessity of renewal—are not isolated to the old industrial regions of the north. And the concepts for revitalizing parish life will be applicable across the board.

Learning from Hippies

There's very little in Church history that's more easily dated than a parish folk band called the Peacemakers. This particular group played for the Saturday vigil Masses at our neighborhood parish through the 1970s; a photo from 1977 features a drum set painted with (of course) a dove and the group's name in that distinctive elongated hippie typeface; floral-print shirts with enormous floppy collars; and hairstyles cribbed directly from *The Brady Bunch*. (The drummer is a dead ringer for Peter Brady.)

Peace was all the rage in the sixties and seventies. As the Vietnam War dragged on for nearly a generation, young hippies saw in their parents a lust for power, sublimated into constricting conventional norms, that manifested itself in militarism and the perpetual competition of the marketplace. Their solution was simple: Embrace the full liberation of the human spirit, the fruit of which will be the end of conflict as we seek and spontaneously arrange the peace we all desire. As Scott McKenzie sang in his ode to the city on the bay: "If you're going to San Francisco / You're gonna meet some gentle people there."

The theory was that peace was more than just the absence of conflict; it was the presence of harmony. And harmony *among persons* depended on harmony *within persons*, which in turn required that each man and woman be able to fulfill his or her deepest desires. At peace with his own spirit, each member of this emergent order could live with the love that makes social peace possible. Peace, therefore, is a *substantive, positive good.* It is also intrinsically related to justice: "No justice," as the protestors say, "no peace."

Now, everything I just said is not only compatible with Catholic thought, but is more or less a restatement of the teaching of St. Thomas Aquinas himself. In his articles on peace, Thomas writes that "man's heart is not at peace, so long as he has not what he wants, or if, having what he wants, there still remains something for him to want, and which he cannot have at the same time."[29] This peace of the heart is what distinguishes true peace from mere "concord," which is the social unity that lacks the orderliness of each soul. And it is justice that "removes obstacles to peace."[30] The hippie vision of genuine peace was actually more real than the bourgeois simulacrum they rebelled against.

It's no secret that the hippie experiment didn't turn out. San Francisco was a mess of drugs and violence, filth and exploitation.

[29] Thomas Aquinas, *Summa Theologica* II-II, q. 29, art. 1.
[30] Ibid., II-II, q. 29, art. 3.

(I love listening to hippie music, but in a melancholic mode: The radical divergence between the ideal and the reality was, regardless of what we might think of the ideal, tragic.) While the hippies might have accidentally sussed out part of the traditional notion of peace, their understanding of desire and love was completely subjective.

For Thomas and the Church, of course, what man ultimately desires, and must love with all his heart, is God. For the hippies, it was whatever you wanted, but mostly pleasure. Total liberation of the passions did not, in fact, usher in peace, but rather chaos: The man enslaved to his passions is not at peace with himself or with God, and this enslavement will necessarily put him in conflict with others and their masters. Peace *does* require social justice, but social justice requires justice to God, or else it's just the powerful asserting their priority over the weak.

But we should remember what the hippies got right. The lesson that anti-hippies — and, I think, a great deal of ex-hippies — took from the experience was that genuine peace is impossible, the naïve dream of the young who had yet to be "mugged by reality," as the neoconservative Irving Kristol put it. The best we can hope for, we are now told, is a weak version of concord, either spontaneously generated by market forces or imposed by state and corporate power. But this denies reality, too, as Thomas and Augustine and so many others have taught: "All things desire peace."[31]

Yes, we desire to be at peace with our communities, with our families, and with ourselves. All of this comes from the desire to be at peace with our Creator. This desire is actualized through the virtue of charity — love of God. This is so much more than the absence of conflict, so much more than the suppression or sublimation of animosity. It's the image of St. John the Beloved at the

[31] Ibid., II-II, q. 29, art. 2.

Last Supper, resting his head on the breast of Jesus (John 13:23). It's that trust in Christ and in Christ's presence in our fellow men that allows us to experience a taste of the eternal rest of heaven right now.

A place of peace is what the parish can be. The Peacemakers were right, even if their aesthetics were wrong. We just need to remember from Whom peace comes, and to Whom it points us.

Open-Door Policy

We live in a peace-starved world. Our lack of peace is not so much about international conflict — though that is part of it — as it is about the insecurity we feel with others and with ourselves. There are the obvious symptoms, such as the opioid crisis and the rise in suicides and the scourge of pornography, all signs of self-hatred and, at the same time, of a retreat into the self and away from our fellow human beings. But there are also trends like trigger warnings and safe spaces that, while they're easily mocked (and easily abused for political purposes), respond to a genuine fragility that seems to be on the rise.

Meanwhile, solidarity is collapsing. The expectation that corporations will show loyalty to employees through the sharing of success and opportunities for advancement is completely gone. The "gig economy" has caused more and more people to hustle from job to job, client to client. And of course it goes without saying that the essential locus of social stability, the family, is struggling to fulfill its purpose. The result of all of this is insecurity, precariousness, and restlessness.

All of this comes from, and feeds into, a fundamental assumption of bad faith in our fellow men. We don't trust anybody — our elites, our bosses, even our friends and family, and especially ourselves. We don't think it's possible to share anything that's really enduring, anything we can feel secure about, with another person: Everything, from consumer transactions to employment to sex, is temporary and contingent, leaving us waiting for the other shoe to drop and expecting to be betrayed. We simply don't think it's possible to live together.

This is the topic we'll take up in much greater detail in the last section of the book. But here, we'll explore how the parish, regardless of size or expectations of decline (or expansion), can be a haven of peace for the faithful—a place of social and spiritual security where we can find rest.

That rest begins with Jesus. There is no substitute for His personal presence. He should be as accessible as is possible and prudent. The feeling of grasping the handle of a church door and finding it locked tight is like a betrayal or a broken promise, like being a child teased by his father's sleight of hand. Jesus is right behind the doors—but we can't see Him, can't rest with Him.

I understand why church doors are often locked. Of course there's the threat of sacrilege: An accessible Jesus can be abused nearly as easily as He can be adored. I think the threat is overstated, and some simple countermeasures can minimize it further, but more importantly we shouldn't let fear on His behalf overwhelm our duty on His behalf.

More commonly, doors are locked due to insurance regulations: Vandalism of an unlocked church will be blamed on the "negligent" caretakers. On the one hand, the soul of one seeker who wanders into an unlocked church and is saved by his encounter with Christ is worth a million denied burglary claims. On the other hand, pastors are accountable for preserving the material patrimony of the church under their jurisdiction, and their concerns shouldn't be dismissed out of hand. But, as far as possible, the tension should be resolved in favor of openness to the people, and to the promptings of the Spirit that might lead them inside.

The Prodigal Church

My college's chapel—an ecumenical but cathedral-style space in which the Blessed Sacrament was reserved—was always a source of great comfort for me. While it wasn't open twenty-four hours a day, it was reliably open from the early morning through the evening for tourism or for prayer. The university paid students to be "chapel watchers"—one of the plum campus jobs—which entailed sitting at a table in the vestibule so the building was never empty. They would be responsible for giving directions to confused visitors and for notifying the relevant authorities if anything unexpected happened, but the job almost exclusively meant quietly reading or doing homework in a church for a few hours.

If accessibility is made a priority, even a small parish could spare volunteers—or pay a small stipend—to man the church building during consistent hours, and into the night if possible. This would be especially fruitful if the church receives regular foot traffic, but Jesus calls motorists, too. The parish church shouldn't feel like a business or office that keeps convenient hours only: It is a wellspring of grace to the faithful and to the wider community, and we should present it to the world as such. This, more than awkward forced greetings before Mass, makes for a welcoming church, a haven of peace.

Place of Grace

The peace and welcome of Christ, then, should imbue the entire culture of the parish. Like academia and local government, Catholic parishes have a reputation for fostering behind-the-scenes drama: backbiting and conniving and social climbing. It's something we often chuckle at and brush off, but we shouldn't. While there will always be a certain amount of jockeying in any institution, big or small, the parish claims to be the home of Jesus Christ, and should act like it.

One of the benefits of third places is that they tend to be places where social status doesn't matter. If this is true of the barber shop, how much more can and should it be true of the place where the heavenly liturgy and sacraments are celebrated? The sociologists will call this "democratizing," but we don't have to accept that framing: We can call it "Christianizing," where each member of the congregation is recognized first for his identity in Christ, and everything else is secondary.

A friend told me once about a conversation he had with an Episcopalian businessman who chose to go out of his way to attend a posh parish. The businessman said, as if it were the most obvious thing in the world, "I don't want to go to church with my plumber." While this little story plays into certain denominational stereotypes, this spirit can absolutely infect Catholic parishes as well. A proposal in my diocese to merge a notably wealthy suburban parish with several working-class urban parishes was scuttled due to the mutual, explicitly class-based animosity between the congregations: "We don't want to be with them," on the one hand and "We don't want to be with them because we can tell they don't want to be with us," on the other.

This is, to put it kindly, the spirit of decline, not the spirit of renewal. More starkly, it's the spirit of the world rather than the spirit of grace. It's grace that makes community possible—but we have to cooperate with it. We have to respond to the invitation, which is implicit in the very reality of the Mass as a communal act of worship, to let our frustrations and prejudices and anxieties about other people be healed. The parish will not be a place of peace, but rather just another locus of insecurity and instability, indistinguishable from the rest of our culture, until it is a place of grace.

To this end, the pastor must play the essential role of peacemaker. Dysfunction in the social life of the parish is just as serious as dysfunction in the family, and it ultimately rests on the father to set the tone. The internal workings of every parish, like those of every family, are different. We could talk, for instance, about the authority of the priest and the filial piety of the laity, but these take on a nearly infinite variety of appearances depending on culture and personality and even law. Rather, let us just say this: The pastor, through the example of his life, especially the discipline of celibacy, orients his flock toward their final goal. Like Mary, even in the humdrum everyday responsibilities of life, he always points to Jesus.

In so doing, the pastor emphasizes the distinctly *spiritual* nature of the parish. Like the Church, which has a charitable function but isn't an NGO, the parish has a social function but isn't a community center. We've seen this taken to the extreme in the Church of England, which has installed spiral slides and mini-golf courses in its churches to "revitalize" them. It's like scooping the ricotta out of a cannoli and replacing it with tofu. More seriously, it's a grotesque use of sacred space and the erasure of Jesus Christ: A community without Christ is no longer a church at all.

Part of being a center of life and a haven of peace, though, is hosting events and organizations that are not strictly part of the liturgical life of the parish. The parish should be a home away from home not just in the sense that it's a sanctuary for prayer, but in the sense that it's a place where you spend time, where serendipitous meetings happen, where you can just *be*, without expectation or anxiety. I've written some of this book, for instance, sitting in an old school cafeteria while my daughter participates in a scouting group. Other parents mingle, and the smaller kids play, and it's just normal for everyone to hang out at the parish.

This should be understood—and emphasized by the pastor—as part of the *supernatural* mission of the parish. Even when it's for a kids' club instead of Mass, the parish is bringing us together *in Christ* in a way the library or coffee shop, as valuable as they are, does not. Little things set the tone: Opening and closing meetings in prayer, offering opportunities for confession or to pray the Liturgy of the Hours, or the pastor's simply being a priestly presence among his flock.

As the parish grows into a place of peace for the faithful, it will soon feel more feasible to reach out to the community beyond. This, too, is essential to a parish that fulfills God's purpose: being salt and light to the world through Christ-like service, in body and soul.

Works of Mercy

Peace, according to St. Thomas Aquinas, is the fruit of charity: When we love God our souls are in their proper order, and we feel at rest. So, too, will social peace result from truly loving others out of our love of God. A community united in charity is a community united in peace.

But there is, as we said above, another prerequisite to peace, and that is justice. In justice, we give to each according to his due — beginning with our duties to God in the form of religion, and continuing to our duties to our fellow men based on their inalienable dignity. Justice is the duty of all men, but it is particularly the duty of the Christian, who in Christ is given an example of selfless service and through grace is given the fortitude to follow Him. To be a *comprehensive* haven of peace, then, the parish must also be a locus of justice.

Temporal justice can be commutative or distributive: The former regards relationships among members of the community, and the latter the allocation of the commonweal — the shared material goods of the community. While the parish might play some role in the former, for instance by arbitrating disputes among parishioners, its primary outward-facing participation in justice will be distributive. Specifically, this will entail addressing, in some small way, the structural injustice of the surrounding society and economy.

The parish should be a place where the marginalized—the poor, the migrant, the mentally ill—can always go and be assured of being treated with dignity. It should be a place where no one, from a parishioner who's fallen on hard times, to a frightened pregnant woman, to an El Salvadoran migrant, should feel ashamed to ask for help. This doesn't mean that every parish has to become a full-scale social service agency, ready to address every possible need. But every parish should be ready to welcome *any person* who shows up, even if just with a smile and a referral to a trusted organization.

To the extent possible, though, that welcome should go deeper: a food pantry or a soup kitchen; a pay-what-you-can café or a few clean beds and a shower; a place simply *to be* without fear or judgment. This is the parish as an island of dignity in a world of exploitation, an island of rest in a world of hustle, an island of security in a world of precarity. This is the parish as *sanctuary*—not just of Jesus in the Blessed Sacrament, but Jesus in the poor. If the marginalized don't feel welcome, then neither does Christ, and His presence in the tabernacle becomes one of judgment rather than healing.

I know that there are any number of reasons—financial, legal, administrative, bureaucratic, and so on and so forth—that these ideas might be impractical. But businesses and other organizations overcome similar barriers to execute their strategic plans every day. If a group of creative and skillful people believes something is really worthwhile, it can get it done. And I know that this kind of welcome involves risk: to reputation, to property, even to persons. But fear of the consequences of following Christ, maybe more than anything, is the enemy of renewal.

The parish, after all, is the natural place where the corporal works of mercy are performed. The parish has a fuller understanding of the community's needs, and a fuller ability to coordinate a response to them, than any individual or family does. This is, simply, part of what it means to be the local instantiation of the Church.

And of course, as we've said, this duty of justice will be put into action in different ways and with different levels of intensity in every parish community. But a renewed Church is one where the general public knows that the Catholic parish, whether in a booming suburb or a rusty city neighborhood, is a place of refuge, a place where the regular rules of fear and insecurity don't apply, a place where the reality of Christ's presence in the Eucharist is manifested in bold service and unselfish love.

The Big Picture

In the introduction, we discussed then Fr. Joseph Ratzinger's remarkable 1969 diagnosis of the Church's future. Let's return to one section in particular:

> From the crisis of today the Church of tomorrow will emerge
> — a Church that has lost much. She will become small and
> will have to start afresh more or less from the beginning.
> She will no longer be able to inhabit many of the edifices
> she built in prosperity. As the number of her adherents diminishes, so it will lose many of her social privileges. In
> contrast to an earlier age, it will be seen much more as a
> voluntary society, entered only by free decision. As a small
> society, it will make much bigger demands on the initiative
> of her individual members.[32]

We're seeing this play out every day in shrinking dioceses. When Pittsburgh's current spasm of contraction is complete, we'll have

---

[32] Ratzinger, *Faith and the Future.*

about five dozen parishes left, most with multiple "campuses," down from 444 parishes in the 1930s. It's no longer possible to have truly neighborhood parishes within walking distance, and we can no longer count on a Catholic culture to keep upcoming generations tethered to the Church. Nothing will come easily: We'll have to go to battle for every soul.

It's good to realize this, though, and to be shaken out of our complacency. Dioceses that are thriving, at least in terms of the number of people in the pews, should take note: You can't count on culture without genuine discipleship. I talked to a priest friend who's regarded as something of a parish-turnaround artist, and one idea he offered for genuinely accompanying souls deeper into the Faith really struck me: non-sacramental "decision points" or moments of commitment.

While those who are entering the Church have a scheduled baptism and, sometimes, confirmation, a lapsed or lukewarm Catholic tentatively returning to practicing the Faith can float more or less indefinitely. For me, it was a barn-burning homily on sin that motivated me to get back to confession and be reconciled with the Lord, but something a bit more formal can help people to feel as though they're making progress. We're not talking about an evangelical altar call exactly, but that's the general concept: an opportunity to tell yourself, and maybe the wider community, that you're *doing this*. It could be an act of consecration to the Blessed Mother or to the Sacred Heart of Jesus, both beautiful Catholic traditions, or it could be a new rite — that kind of innovation within tradition I'm so fond of.

This is the kind of thinking that needs to be applied not just to staunch the bleeding in declining regions, but to act as a prophylactic in growing ones. Even in regions that give the appearance of vitality, the missionary spirit of the smaller, bolder, more agile Church should be cultivated. I agree with Fr. Ratzinger: While there is and will continue to be much to mourn, there is also a certain liberation in our shedding of institutions and prestige. We are freer to be boldly creative, to practice fearless authenticity, and most of all to emphasize Christ without hesitation or apology.

The truth is that the future of the parish in regions like mine is not clear. I don't think it'll get to the point where just a few priests are "riding the circuit," as they did on the eighteenth-century frontier, visiting each parish every few weeks. But the old model of the neighborhood parish—even the suburban neighborhood parish—is dying out and being replaced by multi-campus regional parishes. It's much harder to be the center of life when close prox-imity is all but out of the question, and catalyzing community takes more-direct effort. There are no easy solutions.

In spite of these challenges, which can seem overwhelming from our limited point of view, we can echo Fr. Ratzinger's godly optimism:

> But in all of the changes at which one might guess, the Church will find her essence afresh and with full conviction in that which was always at her center: faith in the triune God, in Jesus Christ, the Son of God made man, in the pres-ence of the Spirit until the end of the world. In faith and prayer she will again recognize the sacraments as the wor-ship of God and not as a subject for liturgical scholarship.[33]

As long as parish life relentlessly directs people to Christ, it can-not fail. And the fundamental place this happens is in the liturgy.

---

[33] Ibid.

6

Living Liturgically

Inescapable

Kanye West isn't the first celebrity musician to undergo a public conversion to Christianity. Forty years earlier, Bob Dylan entered his Evangelical period, during which he won a Grammy for "Gotta Serve Somebody." The refrain included these lines:

> Well, it may be the devil or it may be the Lord,
> But you're gonna have to serve somebody.

In response, John Lennon released a parody, "Serve Yourself," which, besides being profane and blasphemous, missed the mark by being more angry than funny. The refrain went like this:

> You got to serve yourself,
> Ain't nobody gonna do it for you.

In a spoken-word addendum later in the song, Lennon asked, "Who else is gonna do it for you? / It ain't me I tell you that." The ex-Beatle was, of course, too much of a nitwit to understand that his framing didn't undermine Dylan's at all, but rather affirmed and extended it. "Serving yourself" doesn't eliminate the master-servant dynamic; rather, in trying to reject all exterior masters, we become enslaved to our passions, which are at least as jealous as any other master. There's no escaping service: The question is always, Whom do we serve?

What Lennon's "Serve Yourself" does undercut, though, is his own rhetoric about the universal brotherhood of mankind. It's pretty hard for "the world to live as one," as he annoyingly lilted at the end of "Imagine," when everyone's focused on fulfilling his own desires. Universal fraternity is comprehensible only in the context of a shared supernatural lineage; universal solidarity is possible only in fulfillment of a shared supernatural purpose. "Imagine" denies the legitimacy of anything intrinsically shared among persons, especially supernaturally, then exhorts us to, well, share everything. It's a kind of distinctly modern stupidity that would have been ridiculed by all the previous generations we portray as benighted and ignorant.

But Lennon won. "Imagine" is still a radio staple, and while "Serve Yourself" is only a curiosity, its ethos consumes our culture. Even as cynicism about the possibility of real brotherhood has taken root, Lennon's self-contradictory ideal of total personal liberation as the path to social peace is still the prevailing assumption, especially among the cultural elite. Whether in matters of money or matters of sex, we're taught that we serve others best by serving ourselves first. It's the anti-gospel.

In winning, though, Lennon has proved Dylan right. The result of his brand of liberalism hasn't been liberation from service, but the proliferation of new masters. That is, freedom from an all-loving God frees us only to join the service of far more jealous and less compassionate masters: Around us, there are corporations and the state, political parties and consumer brands, exacting identities to perform and social media cliques to please; within us there are lust and greed, pride and resentment, anxiety and self-hatred. The opposite of true faith isn't atheism but idolatry; if we don't serve God, we'll serve any number of gods of our own making.

Service is inescapable, in other words, because religion is inescapable. Religion is much more than a curious sociological phenomenon or any subjective set of supernatural beliefs; fundamentally it is the virtue by which we justly fulfill our duties to our place in society and creation. The question isn't whether we are "religious," but whether we are succeeding or failing at these duties, and thus at the virtue of religion.

The pagan Romans had a concept of *religio* just as surely as Christians did, based on things like properly honoring the emperor and properly propitiating the gods. As the venerable Cicero explained, authentic religion was distinct not only because it was socially valuable, but because it fulfilled one's own nature and thus brought happiness. What was *good* was also *advantageous*. The Church extended this understanding of *religio* to a Heavenly Father, rather than just the fatherland: In the virtue of religion we place ourselves properly in the order of creation by treating God, the transcendent Other, with complete love and prescribed worship. Thus we fulfill our nature and, through His grace, become more like Him until He receives us into perfect and eternal communion with Him in heaven. What is *good* is also *advantageous*.

Every person, even the most thoroughgoing "atheist," makes decisions about his life based on what he believes to be true about his place in the universe, what will fulfill his purpose, and what will make him happy. And so we all perform duties in service of our notion of truth: If we think money is the most important thing, we pursue promotions and raises and deals to the exclusion of other goods; if we think pleasure is the most important thing, we pursue sex and power and (again) money to the exclusion of other goods; if we think Jesus is the most important thing, we pursue holiness above all other goods. The question, then, is whether our idea of truth is right or wrong—whether we worship the true God or cheap knockoffs. And when the true God recedes in importance within a soul or a community, the knockoffs fill the vacuum.

Competing Liturgies

Ritual, any anthropologist will tell you, is part of every human community. Secular scientists will give you any number of materialist explanations for this fact, but they all miss the simple truth: God built ritual into our nature, because it is through ritual—specifically, through liturgy—that we worship Him the way He asks us to: "Do this in remembrance of me" (Luke 22:19).

But liturgy is, of course, not an innovation of the New Covenant. The Old Testament is full of examples of ritual and liturgical worship. Abraham's interrupted sacrifice of Isaac was a ritual. The Passover was a ritual. The Psalms were liturgical songs. In Exodus and Leviticus, God delivered precise instructions on everything from the construction of the tabernacle to the arrangement of worship to the vestments of the priests. We could go on, but the point is clear: God made us to glorify Him, and the primary way we do so is through liturgy.

Like anything that's built into our nature, though, liturgy can be misdirected. There are the obvious examples of occult rituals and Black Masses. More frequently, though, our ersatz liturgies look like, say, professional sporting events. Professional football, especially since it generally takes place on the Sabbath and increasingly replaces genuine worship, is a great example.

NFL games and their broadcasts follow a precise set of rules and are therefore predictable from week to week. First there's the order of events: a pregame show with interviews and predictions; the introductions of the broadcasters followed by kickoff; regularly spaced commercial breaks and a halftime of exactly twelve minutes; the final score and a sign-off. (*Ite missa est.*) The players and officials wear prescribed, identifying clothing proper to their roles and authority, including the badges worn by team captains. In the stadium there are some prescribed postures, such as standing for the national anthem, which functions as a kind of benediction, and *definitely not* standing if everyone else is sitting. Like a church's windows and statuary, the stadium is filled with symbols honoring the venerable benefactors of the liturgy—Staples and Heinz and the Home Depot. You get the idea.

The problem isn't the simple fact that professional sports take on the form of a liturgy—that's completely natural, even good. There's definitely a problem with what and whom the liturgies venerate: The whole thing has become an oblation to consumer capitalism. But more importantly, the problem is in what they *replace*. Pop culture liturgies are fine as far as they go, but they have exploded in number and popularity and intensity just as the genuine liturgies of the Lamb of God have declined. This is not a coincidence.

We'll talk more about the specifics of the Mass later, but here let's focus on a specific way the Mass should function in our lives: as a fulcrum in the organization of our time. The Mass is to be the fixed point around which everything else is organized. Even if we sometimes go to Sunday Mass at different time than usual, *we still go to Sunday Mass*, and we arrange things as best we possibly can to make that happen. (There's something to be said for *reducing* the number of options to force the faithful to commit, but with the proliferation of weekend labor there are also real benefits to keeping several options so those with unchosen Sunday duties can attend.)

The alternative to organizing our time around the Mass is not complete freedom. Put differently, Sunday Mass is not an imposition on what is by nature unstructured time. Someone or something always has a claim on us: It's just a question of whose claims we recognize, and when. A weekend "free" of Mass (barring compulsory work or illness) will always be a weekend dedicated to things we consider more important than Mass: professional sports, or travel, or concerts, or planning a party, or resting because we've exhausted ourselves during the rest of the week.

The same goes for the entire liturgical calendar. The alternative to observing the Church's fasts, feasts, holy days of obligation, seasons of penance, and so on, is not an unstructured or liberated life. The alternative is observing the civil-corporate calendar[34] and all its fasts (there aren't very many — bad for business), feasts (Super Bowl Sunday), holy days of obligation (Fourth of July), and seasons of penance (Black History Month). Again, none of these is *bad* in its proper proportion: Shared cultural touchstones such as sporting events are part of living in a society; well-ordered displays of patriotism are expressions of the virtue of piety; if anything, Black History Month unjustly isolates our acknowledgement of racial injustice to a single month when we should be doing far more consistent penance. But they have a habit of becoming disordered, in terms of their importance and their substance, when they are asked to bear more weight than they should.

The point, to be very clear, is not that we should follow the Church's liturgical calendar to the exclusion of the civil-corporate calendar. The point is that *no matter what, we follow a liturgical calendar*. The question is which celebrations we recognize and elevate, and which we downgrade and ignore. It isn't "neutral," for example, to spend January 1 at home recovering from the activities of December 31 without going to Mass; it's choosing to observe our culture's New Year's Day and not the Church's Solemnity of Mary, the Mother of God.

---

[34] I call it the "civil-corporate" calendar rather than simply the civil calendar because the prevailing schedule is more than just a series of federal holidays: It's influenced by a totalizing corporate culture that respects nothing but efficiency and profit, the Sabbath be damned.

The fact that I have to say these things at all demonstrates the extent to which Catholic culture has been dissipated over the past few generations. More than any other institution in the Church, including the family, it's the parish that can push back, renewing the everyday commitment to the Lord that comes with prioritizing *His* claim on our time.

Catholic Unity

The way we organize our time is more about *whom* than *when*: whom we spend time with and whom we share experiences with. For instance, prioritizing your favorite hockey team over the Oscars is a decision about which community you identify with and wish to share experiences with: the wider world of film buffs and poseurs, or your local fan base. Choosing a night at the pub with your friends over your child's first-birthday party says something about how you value your relationship with the guys over your (soon-to-be-lost) relationship with your family.

The parish is the local instantiation of our family in God. If it succeeds in nothing else, it must be — because by its very nature it is — a liturgical community. Liturgy is, quite simply, the communal prayer of the people of God. It is where we experience communion twice over: communion with the Body of Christ as His people, and communion with the Holy Trinity in prayer and the sacraments. It is in liturgy, more than in any number of successful ministries or apostolates, that we recognize, manifest, and participate in the unity of the Church.

Liturgy unites us with our fellow Catholics through space and time.[35] We hear the same readings at Mass as our brethren in Tokyo

---

[35] The Extraordinary Form of the Mass emphasizes the unity through time at the expense, for the moment, of the unity through space:

The Prodigal Church

or the terrorized Church in Nigeria. We pray the same Gloria and Sanctus and Agnus Dei that Christians have prayed for centuries, even if the language and musical settings have changed. And most importantly, in the Mass we share in the same Body and Blood of Christ, the victim of Calvary whose sacrifice unites all who take up their crosses and follow Him.

Expanding the liturgical offerings of the parish expresses and deepens this unity. Having more opportunities to be together not just as a community but as a *praying community* emphasizes the supernatural reality of the Church in her local form: The parish isn't just a group of people committed to the material good of one another, or even of the wider community, but to the *supernatural* common good. When we join our prayers not only with those of our fellow parishioners but with the prayers of our fellow Catholics everywhere, it makes clear the wonderful truth that we're all in this together, helping each other to heaven with Christ as our shared foundation.

This is about more than the Mass: The Church's tradition of liturgical prayer goes beyond the Eucharistic celebration. For inspiration (if not for imitation) we can look to the Curé d'Ars, St. John Vianney. Sunday at Fr. Vianney's parish was grueling. A three-hour Mass, including processions and a lengthy homily, ended in the late morning. After a respite, presumably for some midday nourishment, a catechesis from the pastor—ostensibly for children but well attended by adults—began in the early afternoon. The rest of the day was full of liturgical prayer: Vespers (Evening

---

The different lectionary and calendar were the biggest hurdles for my family to join an Extraordinary-Form parish. This is a perfectly legitimate trade-off, but I pray for a time when we have to sacrifice neither.

Prayer), Compline (Night Prayer), and the Rosary. For every part of Sunday prayer and lessons, the church was full.

We don't have to commit to twelve-hour church days to learn from the patron saint of parish priests. As we dial back expectations, though, we should remember that nineteenth-century France was hardly more secular than twenty-first-century America. While the modern ideology of secularism was not as deeply rooted, St. John Vianney served a community only a generation or so removed from the most violent anti-Catholic cultural and political struggle in history. When he arrived in Ars-sur-Formans, the town parish was moribund and the people disconnected from God and the life of His Church. He didn't waltz into a plum situation and spruce it up; he transformed the parish and, in turn, the town.

Introducing more liturgical prayer in the distracted era of the smartphone might seem extravagant, but we don't have to start with the full Vianney. For instance, Morning Prayer or Lauds could be seamlessly inserted before or after a morning daily Mass, or Vespers attached to an evening Mass. While this kind of public prayer should be open to all in any case, especially families with young children, a weekly or monthly opportunity for Vespers with childcare would signal openness to the entire community. The Liturgy of the Hours, after all, was never meant to be a private prayer just for priests. As the number of clergy declines and loneliness increases, opportunities to pray with the parish community would further integrate the priest and his flock.[36]

---

[36] Lest this seem like a traditionalist point: I am indebted to the liberal Catholic writer Michael Sean Winters for his suggestion of attaching the Liturgy of the Hours to Mass, and for his observation about priestly isolation. See "The Average Day of a Parish Priest," *NCR Today* (blog), *National Catholic Reporter*, June 30, 2009. https://www.ncronline.org/blogs/ncr-today/average-day-parish-priest. The clericalist elevation of the priest to a different plane of existence,

The Prodigal Church

Increasing options for public, communal prayer feels unrealistic because it so contradicts the spirit of the age, which is consumed by busyness, distraction, and isolation. But this is precisely why it's so important: It has always been by embracing the contradictions of Christ—not in a showy or aggressive way, but simply as part of everyday life, as if it's the most natural thing in the world—that the Church has attracted the alienated, the disheartened, the curious, all those who are not well served by the world as it is. The parish, at its best, can demonstrate a different and striking way of simply being in the world.

Being in the World

There's a way of being in the modern world that we perceive to be normal and natural, and it goes something like this: rushing from place to place to meet our work or other "practical" responsibilities, spending downtime either obsessing over those responsibilities or mindlessly scrolling online in order to distract ourselves from them, fitting in friends and family in the interstices, and maybe carving out an hour a week for God. But, as we stressed at the beginning of chapter 3, *being* is necessarily about relationship with the living God. Living as if He doesn't exist, or is indifferent to our existence and what we make of it, may be "normal" these days, but it's not natural, and it's not neutral.

There's no neutral way to be in the world. We're either performing our duties to God and our fellow men, or we're not. We're either living in and reflecting His light to others, or we're absorbing it into our own darkness and denying it to others. We're either growing closer to Him, or we're receding from Him. And when the parish

---

at least in terms of the social life of the Church, will no longer be tenable as there are fewer priests to share this plane.

and its proper orientation toward the Lord recede from our personal and community consciousness, the rest of the world rushes in.

At its very best, the parish can be a node of a better, more *real* way of being in the world—one where our relationship with Christ is always front and center. If the allocation of our time is more about *who* than *when*, then the parish can fulfill its supernatural purpose best by being a place where the people of God can be together with our Lord as much as possible. The parish can make it more visibly possible to organize our lives around Him by offering communal chances to do so.

A simple way to do this, in addition to incorporating the Liturgy of the Hours in some way, is to integrate the liturgical calendar more concretely into parish life. Solemnities and patronal feasts should play a greater role in the lives of the faithful than Presidents' Day or Columbus Day, and this begins with the parish's treating them as more important. It's about more than the vestment color and the Propers of the Mass—though educating the faithful about these would be a good hook. It's about making the parish a place where these feasts can be *really celebrated*, liturgically and socially.

This could begin simply by making the liturgical calendar a priority in communications with parishioners. The faithful should be at least as aware of the upcoming liturgical feasts, and the opportunities to celebrate them at the parish or at home, as they are of the upcoming Boy Scout bake sale. In fact, pegging fundraisers and other parish events to feasts rather than to convenience is a simple pious practice that gently emphasizes the supernatural and acknowledges the saintly assistance that makes all our efforts profitable. Placing the annual parish festival on or near the parish's patronal feast—including a special Mass and the feast's office of prayers—rather than the date considered maximally profitable is a small act of faith that the patron is more than a mascot.

The Prodigal Church

The parish's invitations to the outside world should also be about more than its "secular" offerings. Integrating Mass and the Liturgy of the Hours into these events is a way to consecrate them, but the parish should also communicate its distinctly spiritual offerings to the wider community. In this way, again, it manifests its supernatural purpose and invites the world to more than an encounter with a healthy human community, which is a necessary but an insufficient condition of evangelization. Rather, the parish must invite the world to an encounter with Christ.

Many years ago our Pittsburgh neighborhood was home to the region's Maronite Catholic parish; the church has moved to the suburbs, but a disproportionate number of Arab Christians still live in the area, including the owners of a celebrated Lebanese bakery and café. Recently relics of the Lebanese mystic St. Sharbel passed through town, and the parish hosted an opportunity for veneration of the relics and Eucharistic adoration. Instead of communicating this through distinctly Catholic channels, the parish produced fliers, featuring a glorious monstrance and the hooded visage of the saint, and placed them in the windows of several shops in our neighborhood. This was a parish that communicated its distinctive offering to the world—what it can offer that no other community or institution can. And in a simple way it made Christ present in the everyday life of the neighborhood.

My dream would be for it to be normal for parishioners to spend time at least once a week at the parish for a liturgical or para-liturgical event other than Sunday Mass—a party or seminar or fundraiser pegged to a feast. This is obviously a stretch goal, especially in places where numbers of priests and parishioners are dwindling. But we need goals that, like heaven itself, sometimes feel unreachable to orient us in the right direction. And ultimately a renewed Church is one where parish life demonstrates that it is possible, through grace, to live oriented first toward the Lord, not toward the next promotion or hookup or election.

Foundation or Capstone?

I talked to a parish priest about this vision, and I immediately felt silly as I thought of the day-to-day challenges of his ministry — especially amid the parish mergers that are taking place around our diocese. The idea of convincing already overburdened parishioners not just to show up more than once a week, but to dedicate the resources, in time and money, to make it possible, seemed fantastical.

He didn't disagree with the vision, but emphasized that in his experience liturgical enhancements are the *result* of successful discipleship, not *drivers* of it. In other words, the faithful have to get to the point where they actually desire to live liturgically before implementation can be successful.

This contrasts somewhat with the view among some Catholics, especially traditionalists, that embracing the Church's liturgical patrimony, whether in terms of fasts and feasts or in terms of the form of the Mass, is an essential precursor to renewal. I'm going to take the easy way out on this one and say that liturgy is both the foundation and the capstone of renewal, depending on how we look at it.

First, my priest friend is absolutely right that the success, in terms of attendance, of new liturgical offerings depends on having enough parishioners who are willing to make the time for them. Reorganizing our schedules, including adjusting or giving up habits, feels like a huge commitment — even though once we form new habits they quickly feel totally normal, and it becomes hard to remember how things were before. And the fact of the matter is that, after generations of dissipation of our spiritual and liturgical patrimony, to most of the faithful these kinds of events feel strange and foreign. We've gone native: Like a fish that doesn't understand that it lives in water because it knows nothing else, we're so accustomed to organizing our lives around the civil-corporate calendar and the ever-changing requirements of our economy and culture that doing so feels natural.

And so we need that training in discipleship that authors such as Sherry Weddell have written about so passionately. The first step to choosing Jesus is desiring Him — most specifically, understanding that by our very nature we desire Him because we desire our ultimate happiness. Then we need to be primed for the "next steps," which will be different for every person: For some it will be sacramental or canonical — returning to confession or resolving an illicit marriage — while for others it will be moral or familial — growing in a particular virtue, rooting out a vice, or healing relationships.

In every case the parish, in the person of the priest and competent lay ministers, can be there to provide genuine Christian accompaniment, as Pope Francis has emphasized. This is the authentic rule of gradualism, by which a person comes to know Christ and to amend his life rarely all at once, but usually through a slowly enhanced understanding of what Christ is calling him to be. One of the hardest, but I think most fruitful, aspects of that growth for many people will be arranging the rhythm of life around the liturgical life of the Church. This is liturgy as capstone.

And yet we must insist, first of all, that there are more people ready for that step — who desire to be filled and formed by liturgy right away, for whom it would actually be a *first step* because it suits their lives and their spirituality — than we might think. Liturgy can and must be part of training in discipleship. Expanding liturgical offerings and generally bringing parish life more in accord with the logic and drama and rhythm of the liturgical calendar make

Christ's living presence among us feel more real, which makes following Him feel more realistic. Liturgical living makes the fullness of the Christian life appear more credible because it demonstrates publicly the commitment to organize life around communion with Him and with His people.

Thus prioritizing the nature of the parish as a liturgical community is both part of and a primary goal of any parish discipleship strategy. This becomes especially clear when we remember that, more than anything else, the parish is a fountain of sacramental grace—the grace that makes every other good thing, from community to discipleship to salvation itself, possible.

Fountains of Grace

If the sacraments are the ordinary means by which grace is communicated to the world, and if the parish is the ordinary home of the sacraments, then the parish is the ordinary channel of grace to the people of God—and the entire community. This, more than anything else, is the *purpose* of the parish; everything else depends on it.

It is grace that makes any and all human community possible. I think often about how, in Acts 1:25, the apostles describe the "ministry and apostleship from which Judas turned aside, to go to his own place." Judas's betrayal of Christ was only made worse by his unwillingness to seek forgiveness and to accept the possibility of reconciliation with the community. His going off "to his own place" was a further rejection of Christ and of the healing power of grace.

Without grace, we all go our own way, seeking happiness in lower things and spurning the highest things of all. Without grace, there is no enduring principle of unity that can overcome our squabbling—and whatever temporary principles of unity we can conjure up last only as long as trust remains unbroken. Without grace, there can be no reconciliation with our fellow men because there can be no reconciliation with Christ.

This is why confession is at least as important to the life of the community as the more obviously communal sacraments of Holy Communion and matrimony. The healing grace of this sacrament, which reestablishes and strengthens the relationship between the penitent and the Lord, radiates out into the network of relationships that constitutes and surrounds the parish. Imagine a complex Christmas-light display dependent on a single extension cord plugged into the wall. Each light is a part of our life — a relationship, a responsibility, a ritual — where we have the opportunity to radiate Christ's light and warmth to others. Mortal sin kicks out the plug; the sacrament of confession replaces it, bringing Christ's peace not just to our souls but, in an attenuated but real way, to those whom we interact with at every incandescent node in our lives.

Like enhanced liturgy, frequent opportunities for confession are both essential to discipleship and made more practical by the success of discipleship. But we have to start somewhere. Offering confession, especially at a large parish, during only one half-hour slot per week signals quite clearly to the faithful that it's simply not important: There is absolutely no way everyone who needs the sacrament is able to receive it between 4:47 and 5:12 on a Saturday afternoon. It becomes an optional accessory to parish life, something only the really serious and probably slightly deranged people do. It goes without saying that deemphasizing confession bears rotten fruit not only by increasing the frequency of sacrilegious reception of Communion, but by enhancing the embarrassment of not receiving.

This isn't *Field of Dreams*: If you offer frequent confession times, people may not come. The reestablishment of the norm of confession might take years or decades or longer. (Not every parish priest will be St. John Vianney, who famously would spend sixteen to eighteen hours a day in the box without running out of penitents.) But there's absolutely no chance at all of its being reestablished if the parish doesn't signal the importance of reconciliation by offering multiple convenient options.

This, it seems to me, is the lesson of every opportunity the parish has to be a channel of grace to the community in the way only a Catholic church can, by sacraments and liturgy: If the pastor and lay leaders fail to treat them seriously, no one else will, either. If it's clear that raising money and maintaining stagnant ministries are what the shepherd and his staff care about most, then the faithful will justly wonder, "What's the point?" Money and ministries don't justify themselves: They have to be *for* something—or, better, Someone.

It's grace that transforms all our efforts into something pleasing to the Lord and useful in building up His Kingdom. It's grace that makes the parish into something more than a beautiful building or lovely liturgy, but an alluring, evangelizing community. It's grace that makes the parish an irreplaceable asset not just to local Catholics, but to everyone who comes into contact with it. And so it's in emphasizing the *liturgical* and *sacramental* aspects of its mission that the parish most fully realizes its place in God's order.

Renewal, after all, is first and foremost an action of grace, of allowing God's divine life to flow upon and into us. Nothing will change for the better unless and until we are open to that grace. And it's the distinctive role of the parish not just to be a fountain of grace, but to make the life of grace attractive and available to as many people as possible.

No parish will manifest every attribute we've discussed in these chapters; no parish will be perfect. But every parish can be a place where the transformative power of grace is demonstrated, where the radicalism of the Christian message and way of life is shown to be credible and beautiful. Every parish can be not just a home for Jesus, but a beacon of His light and love and peace.

It is then the distinctive role of the family to be the school of grace, where the fruits of God's divine life are concentrated, passed down, and brought more fully into the world.

Part 4

The Family

7

School of Grace

It Takes a Church

What does it take to raise a child? In 1996, Hillary Clinton famously co-opted an apocryphal African proverb to tell the country that "it takes a village." While her book of that title, in keeping with the Clintons' electoral strategy at that time, was in many places down-right conservative, including paeans to "personal responsibility" and sexual abstinence, the concept of the village-raised child has come into American culture as "nanny-state" liberalism in disguise.

The alternative vision of child-rearing is captured in the title of then senator Rick Santorum's 2005 response: *It Takes a Family.* Like Clinton's book, Santorum's isn't as doctrinaire as it has been perceived: He advocates for a robust pro-family public policy, not an aloof leave-families-alone libertarianism. And yet the concept of the family raised child has come into American culture as an anti-government and sometimes antisocial assertion of the sovereign self-sufficiency of the nuclear household.

And so we've ended up with two rival camps, *village* and *family,* one representing children as the responsibility of a national bureaucracy, and the other representing children as the responsibility exclusively of their parents. Neither one represents the views of the respective book it takes as inspiration. We've shoehorned the family—one of the most potent images of God's love and the surest earthly representation of His relationship with His people—into the restrictive categories of modern American politics. And we're all the worse for it.

If the family is going to be a node of the renewal of the Church —and it absolutely must be—then we must learn again to think about it in God's terms, not those of our secular politics. We must remember that its first purpose is not the rearing of competent citizens or loyal employees or savvy entrepreneurs or any other inputs (or "human resources," a phrase whose ubiquity should convince us we're living in a dystopia) into our dehumanizing, mammon-obsessed regime, but the rearing of saints. We must remember that the most important relationship our children will have is not with the gatekeepers of worldly success, but with Jesus Christ.

This is what the village-versus-family dynamic misses: the essential relationship between the family and Christ. As we said earlier, this relationship is baked into our very nature as created beings, and it manifests itself in the rearing of children just as surely as anywhere. The idea that the nuclear family and the wider community are necessarily *in competition*, though, depends on the assumption that there is no relationship that transcends them and no possible good that can unite them—that is, no common good shared by all, especially the upcoming generation.

The question, then, isn't whether it takes a village or a family—because it takes a church. It takes a church, *the Church*, to unite children and their families and their communities to Christ. It takes the Church, not just as an institution but as the invisible reality that connects us to the communion of heaven and communicates God's grace, to allow families to manifest that unity of purpose by tending to their own proper good while being radically open to the community, both to assist and to be assisted. It takes the Church, not material prosperity or bourgeois respectability or energetic self-sufficiency, to elevate the natural institution of the family to its supernatural end.

Just like every one of us, the family is either moving toward Christ or receding from Him — and no amount of worldly success can make up for a deficit in holiness. The family plays its role in renewing the Church not by fulfilling some 1950s or 1980s or 2010s stereotype of the ideal traditional family, and certainly not by closing in on itself out of fear of vulnerability or a disordered commitment to autonomy, but rather by being open to the grace the Church mediates to and for us. Yes, that means participating in Mass and other aspects of parish life, but it also means consecrating and conforming every aspect of life to God's glory. It means demonstrating, to its own children and the world, a way of life ordered first to heaven.

And so the family that will contribute to the renewal of the Church will neither be obsessed with its own self-sufficiency nor serve as an adjunct of a state-managed society. It will be an integral participant in the life of the Church — and it will be a little church itself.

Little Oratory

I have at times mused about bringing the "spirit of the monastery" into the family home. We have four children under seven years old, so I feel like the coach of the Cleveland Browns musing about winning the Super Bowl. But, for the sake of the example, let me go into a little more detail about what I mean.

When I think of the spirit of the monastery, I think of habits of life where all work is ordered toward the good of the community, and where the good of the community is consecrated to God through a regular and communal prayer life. In the family home, this could take the form of consistently cheerful completion of chores for the common good (don't laugh), and obedience to the rightful authorities directing these tasks (okay, laugh a little)—authorities who themselves participate generously, cheerfully, and patiently in building up the common good (feel free to laugh hysterically). While this vision might seem extravagant, as might the earlier vision of parish life, we must believe it is possible through grace, and we must aim for it—while prudently expecting resistance, most of all from ourselves.

The basis of this vision of shared effort, though, is shared prayer. And this is where my imagination really runs wild. What I envision is a truncated version of the Liturgy of the Hours that includes family prayer roughly every three hours: Morning Prayer or a simple Morning Offering around nine; the Angelus at noon; Midday Prayer or the Divine Mercy chaplet around three; the Angelus again or Vespers around six; and the Rosary or Night Prayer or both before bed. (Just writing this out makes me smile, but when I leave my home office and experience my lovely and, uh, *spirited* children again, I'll forget all about it.)

It's not, on its face, an impossible idea. And I'm lucky enough to be able to work with words for a living, largely from home, so I could help. But of course wrangling the kids just for the daily Rosary can be exhausting—and it took us several years to work up to that. More importantly, though, the life of the family simply cannot be that regimented: There're the vicissitudes of homeschooling and unscheduled visits from friends, the impromptu walks to the ice cream parlor, the emergency errands for diapers, and so on. If anything like this were to be attempted, it would require enough flexibility to account for *life*—and it might be impossible ever to build up the consistency to make it stick.

I think this is why my spiritual director told me to chill out about the monastery idea. But I describe it here to give you permission to dream a little bit. We're not raising little monks and nuns, but we should be raising children for whom the habits of monks and nuns aren't so bizarre or extraordinary that committing to a religious vocation seems impossible. And we must be raising children for whom God is an ever-present reality, not a weekly interloper.

And so, rather than forming a little monastery, maybe we can settle for a *little oratory*. (I'm taking the name from the title of David Clayton and Leila Marie Lawler's book on praying in the home, which I warmly recommend.) This is simply the home as a place of prayer—a place where communion with the Lord is simply part of everyday life.

It might sound simple, but it's downright radical in a world where religion is supposed to take place exclusively in two locations: within the four walls of a church, and inside your own head. One of the biggest stumbling blocks to renewal is the acquiescence of Catholic families to this notion, and the resulting hesitation to imbue family life with religious practices and principles. We act as if the family is a quasi-public, and therefore officially secular space: After all, we're raising kids to go out into that secular space, and we don't want them to be too weird! I remember visiting the home of an Evangelical friend from school and being simultaneously charmed and taken aback by the overtly religious décor: Didn't they know that people might think that was *strange*?

Not only does such a space allow guests to be embraced by the reality of Christ, but more importantly, it normalizes that reality within the family itself. Religious art, regular prayer, impromptu catechesis (don't give secular, "neutral" answers to those questions kids love to ask about life and death!), casually talking about the sacraments as if they're the most normal thing in the world—all these little decisions and habits turn the Faith from a weekly hobby into a lived reality. More than saying that God is real, it's *acting* as if He's real, organizing the home and everyday life as if He's real, that makes that reality not just credible but palpable to children.

The Prodigal Church

This easy familiarity with the Faith in the home is easier for some to come by than for others. It took me years to get used to talking about Jesus — even with fellow Christians, and even with children — without feeling a little embarrassed at sounding trite or guileless. And I still feel more comfortable *writing* about Jesus than I do speaking about Him: It's almost a kind of stammer, a moment of mental resistance that says, "Are you *sure* you're not going to sound like a fool? Are you *sure* you're not going to sound impractical, dreamy, or childish? Are you *sure* you want to be seen as a *Jesus guy?*" The best prophylaxis against this is to make Jesus, in image and word and sacrament, completely normal, from the beginning.

And so even if the spirit of the monastery proves elusive, and even if the spirit of prayer seems, well, a bit of a reach amid squabbling over rosaries or crayons or who gets to say what, we can still count on the spirit of grace that comes from affirming Christ's presence among us. It's that grace, and our openness to it, that will allow the family to become a driver of renewal, forming a new generation with the boldness to see it through.

Openness to Life, Openness to God

In today's world, the most visible aspect of the radicalness of Catholic marriage is the prohibition of artificial contraception. The large families that tend to result from this teaching become both a tangible symbol of the fruitfulness intrinsic to authentic marriage and, often, a signal to others of gritty faithfulness to God.

But here we need to be careful. First, seeing family size as proportional to sanctity is gravely unjust to those with medical or other hardships that place large families — or having children at all — out of reach. The outward faithfulness of these families, as we will soon discuss, lies not in *biological* fruitfulness but in the fruitfulness of their labor (for one another and for good works), of their service, and above all of their friendships. Ultimately, it lies in docility to God's will for them, in whatever form that fruitfulness takes.

In fact, this framing completely misses the point of the openness to life that is written into our nature and the nature of marriage. It's not about making babies with maximal efficiency, like an assembly line. It's not about demonstrating a tenacious determination to rack up virtue points by bringing as many challenging children into your family as possible. And it's certainly not about mimicking some model of the ideal traditional household. All of these shift the emphasis from God to ourselves, elevating our own notions of family — and our own willpower to achieve those goals — over meek cooperation with *His* will.

It's this *docility*, not aggressive countercultural signaling or demonstrations of moral tenacity or even the pursuit of calloused fortitude, that is at the heart of the openness to life. Pope St. Paul VI, amid some of the strongest condemnations of contraception in *Humanae Vitae*, put it this way:

> But to experience the gift of married love while respecting the laws of conception is to acknowledge that one is not the master of the sources of life but rather the minister of the design established by the Creator. Just as man does not have unlimited dominion over his body in general, so also, and with more particular reason, he has no such dominion over his specifically sexual faculties, for these are concerned by their very nature with the generation of life, of which God is the source. (13)

We are not the *masters*, but the *ministers* of life. It is not up to us independently to decide precisely where or when or how new life will be joined to our own lives, but rather to ensure the conditions to make new life possible are met, and to respond faithfully to whatever God ordains. This is the radical lesson of *Humanae Vitae*, and it's much more serious and more difficult than simply filling a minibus with children, which could just as easily be an assertion of our own autonomy as an intentional participation in God's will.

We live in a culture of selfishness and sterility, but the connection between the two isn't as direct as Catholic commentators tend to suggest. When we say that choosing sterility—that is, hijacking one's reproductive and endocrine systems to limit or rule out entirely the possibility of having children—is straightforwardly a result of selfishness, we imply that fecundity is straightforwardly related to selflessness. Besides the selfishness that having several children *always* reveals in parents—leading, God willing, to recognition and healing of that selfishness—the choice to aim for a large family can itself be selfish. This way of life could be chosen, for instance, as a form of conspicuous consumption (demonstrating how many children can be lavished with goodies and sent to the best schools) or even to exploit the children's labor as they, and their parents, age. But even more insidiously, it can be an example of spiritual pride, of accumulating virtue and hardship points to show everyone else just how dogged one's faithfulness is—when in fact it's not faithfulness at all, but conceit.

So it's not about a simple correlation between selfishness and sterility. Rather, it's about *autonomy*—the idea that what makes us most fully human is our complete independence, our ability to order our lives entirely as we see fit. Autonomy, in turn, requires *control*. And control requires *predictability*. And nothing more seriously endangers the predictability of our lives, and thus our present and future autonomy, than fertility. *This*, not simple selfishness, is why we sterilize ourselves. It's the lust for control—to become masters rather than ministers of life—that is the *first* movement away from God; the actual obstruction of procreation comes down the line.

Our openness to life, then, is judged not by the number of lives but by the extent of our openness to God's *life*—that is, His grace.

Not using artificial contraception is the *beginning* of this openness, not its endpoint. When one perceives openness to life as a lifestyle choice, as an expression of one's own autonomy, or as a demonstration of virility, that's adopting the same posture toward the primacy of human independence that the culture teaches. It might follow God's law strictly speaking, but it does so almost by accident.

The family serves its God-ordained purpose as a school of grace, therefore, by a radical openness to grace — only one aspect of which, though a very important one, is openness to life. Joyless procreation for the sake of competition or performance or demographic duty isn't going to be a credible witness to children, let alone to the wider community, of the deep goodness of Catholic marriage. It will look like anything else in our culture: one lifestyle choice among many, and a rather odd one at that. Weirdness is fine; in fact it's very good, but not for its own sake: It must be joyful weirdness for the sake of the Kingdom, in docile conformity with God's will.

The Catholic family cannot play its part in the renewal of the Church if it is merely acting out God's law without allowing God's life to imbue it. It's about being the place where the life of grace is learned, and specifically where the sacramental grace of the parish is amplified, and its fruits manifested.

Grace-Filled Reality

We live in a graceless world. I don't mean that God has abandoned us, of course — just that we act as though He has. For instance, we organize our political life as if God isn't real, as if the best we can hope for is whatever fallen human beings can conjure. Thus we acquiesce in unacceptable compromises, selling out the unborn, or the migrant, or the poor for the sake of some grand long-term strategy that never seems to pan out. Thus we say that political and economic and military outrages are unavoidable, that they're just the way of the world. Thus we say, and come to believe, that concepts such as "justice" and "mercy" and "peace" are unattainable, childish preoccupations.

In the 1986 film *The Mission*, eighteenth-century Spanish Jesuit missions have brought Christ and peace to the indigenous Guaraní people, but a cardinal has been dispatched from Rome to manage the orderly transfer of the mission lands to Portugal, which sees the Guaraní as good for nothing but slave labor. After a bloody clash in the jungle highlands as colonial forces evict the Jesuits and their charges, the cardinal is crestfallen. He accosts the Portuguese legate: "And you have the effrontery to tell me this slaughter was justified?" The secular authority responds coolly, "We must work in the world, Your Eminence. The world is thus." The cardinal shoots him an angry glance before uttering one of my favorite lines in film: "No, Señor Hontar. Thus have we made the world. Thus have I made it."

We don't have to accept the world "as it is." This is a completely secular framing of human affairs, one that denies the possibility of anything beyond wallowing in our brutishness. The whole point of Christian witness in the world is to bring people to Christ, but *we do that by building up His Kingdom of grace*, even and especially when it seems unreasonable in worldly terms, not by despairing that peace and justice are impossible. Indeed, there is no greater acquiescence in secular ideology than to reject the truth that grace can and will elevate our possibilities.

When we do so, we accept the entire premise of secularism: It doesn't matter if God is real or not. Those who believe in Him are free (within shrinking boundaries) to organize their lives as such, while those who don't believe in Him are free to do the same; but when it comes to public affairs, we act as if the nonbelievers are right. This way of thinking doesn't remain sequestered in the world of politics; it seeps into family life, where it corrodes the channels by which we pass down the Faith through the generations.

The most obvious way this has seeped into family life, even Catholic family life, is the implicit acceptance of the possibility of divorce. We say that Church teaching—that is, the direct words of Jesus Christ—is a nice *ideal*, but unworkable in practice. And so all too often we keep an escape clause in the back of our minds.[37] This is never idle; in subtle ways it affects the way we act toward our spouses, but more importantly it ensures that the spirit of the home does nothing to counteract the ubiquity of divorce and divorce-mindedness in the surrounding culture. By leaving open the door to divorce even just a crack, we allow critical uncertainty to infect children's hearts, and we make a future where divorce is out of the question harder for them to imagine.

Divorce is just the starkest example, though. In everyday life, this despairing of grace manifests itself in innumerable ways, all related to the inability to imagine genuine self-giving. But this is precisely the spirit that must define the family home:

> The relationships between the members of the family community are inspired and guided by the law of "free giving." By respecting and fostering personal dignity in each and every one as the only basis for value, this free giving takes the form of heartfelt acceptance, encounter and dialogue, disinterested availability, generous service and deep solidarity.
>
> Thus the fostering of authentic and mature communion between persons within the family is the first and irreplaceable school of social life, and example and stimulus for the

---

[37] It should go without saying that a genuine escape from abuse is completely licit, and is not the kind of "escape clause" I'm discussing in this section.

The Prodigal Church

broader community relationships marked by respect, justice, dialogue and love.[38]

Here, Pope St. John Paul II envisions the family as leaven for society, forming children in the virtues that make genuine community possible. But too often the process has worked in the other direction: The despairing of the possibility of living together in selfless service, which is fundamentally the despair of God's love and grace, infects the inner life of the family. It is through boldly cooperating with grace by *choosing*, every day, to trust and to be worthy of trust, that we can demonstrate, to our children and to the world, a better way.

Because it's hard to imagine, let alone bring into being, something we've never seen before. You can describe an exotic animal to a child and ask her to draw it, and she might do pretty well; but she'll do better if she can see a picture, and better still if she can touch and interact with the real thing. As true as this is for simple craftsmanship, it's even more salient for ways of life. Our culture gives us no examples of grace-filled living, of attractive communities of mutual service built on prayer, and so we have to create them for our children. Yes, it's about showing them how it's done, but first and foremost, it's about showing them that it's *possible*, even as we make mistakes and fumble around trying to figure out the details.

The family, after all, is where the contours of reality—of what is normal, of what is possible—are first shaped for a child. To return to a theme of this book: There's no neutral way to go about this. Either that reality will be the dominant, secular, graceless one, or it will be the true reality of Jesus Christ and His Church.

It is right here, in these first years of life, that so much of the dissipation of the Faith has taken place. The Church, as the people

[38] Pope St. John Paul II, apostolic exhortation on the family *Familiaris Consortio* (November 22, 1981), no. 43.

of God, became complacent and assumed that families didn't have to work hard to shape their children's reality: Jesus was an obvious presence, and the culture either affirmed this or at least failed to deny it. But things changed, and soon the graceless world of mistrust and cynicism rather than authentic peace and love, the spirit of the quid pro quo rather than the spirit of self-giving, formed the limits of the possible for generations of the faithful.

There are two basic prerequisites to allowing God's grace to renew the Church: We have *to want it*, and we have *to believe it is possible*. Both of these begin in the Catholic family, where a microcosm of the grace-filled world—and of the grace-renewed Church—can be manifested to the next generation. And they can see that it is possible, and that it is good.

Permeability

The reality shaped by the family cannot, of course, be completely self-contained—but this is a good thing. It is neither possible nor desirable for the family to be hermetically sealed off from the outside world.

This permeability is necessarily two-way: The family both absorbs and contributes to its environment. This presents obvious challenges and opportunities, but the challenges needn't induce fear, nor the opportunities apprehension. It is in the very nature of grace to draw us out of ourselves, toward the Holy Trinity, of course, but also toward a confident communion with our fellow man. It is within the security of the family that children learn the self-giving love that grace makes possible; it is then from this security that they learn how to apply that way of being to the rest of the world.

There is no ideal level of the family's permeability to the surrounding culture. For instance, some families will monitor television more strictly than others, and still others will have no television at all. (In the case of personal Internet-connected devices in today's pandemic of pornography, the range of safe options is much narrower.) The important thing is that children learn to discern what media is worthy and what is unworthy, what is dignified and what is undignified. It's not about creating an Edenic preserve from corruption, like a botanical garden where an unspoiled stasis is maintained, but creating a training academy for engaging with modern society.

This might sound intense, but it doesn't have to be. For instance, it might be as simple as sharing our own cultural passions with our children, and using the opportunity to frame them appropriately. I'm not a *Star Wars* fan (I'm a *Star Trek: The Next Generation* man, like my father), but several of our friends are, and they are passing down that interest to their children. They aren't doing so uncritically—they discuss the films' aesthetic and moral deficits, and so on—but neither are they sucking all the fun out of it: *Star Wars* is a genuine and (mostly) worthy part of our civilization, and it's natural to participate thoughtfully in it. The family is the place where the *thoughtfully* part can get worked out, so kids can be inoculated against being entranced by mindless amusements.

Most of all, it's about forming habits of family life that incline children, and everyone for that matter, toward a Christ-like posture toward the surrounding world—neither fearful nor brazen, neither contemptuous nor uncritical. This might include more or less restrictive media habits, but more importantly it includes such things as habits of kindness and service and hospitality. It means speaking with the same warmth to a transgender clerk at Wendy's as to a maître d' at a posh restaurant. It means giving freely and easily to the needy who cross our paths. It means regularly welcoming the awkward youngster from a broken home down the street for dinner. This leaning into the world is possible and prudent, though, only if the family is securely anchored to heaven in prayer.

We all know that Jesus was fearless in welcoming the physically and morally corrupted, but He also retreated to the wilderness to get away from it all, to recharge in the presence of His Heavenly Father. He didn't have to do this, but that's what makes it all the more notable as an example: He demonstrated the importance of *both* openness to others *and* retreat into security. But, importantly, this retreat isn't about self-obsession, but the higher communion with the Lord that makes our vulnerable openness feasible and fruitful.

It is anathema to a certain view of fatherhood especially, but vulnerability is an essential part of reflecting God's grace to the world, and of building a family culture that contributes to renewing the Church. Holiness, whether personal or communal, is never without risk. And it is holiness, above all else and at all costs, that the Church and the world she is called to save need. This doesn't mean throwing our doors open to any and all persons and influences, but it does mean that erring on the side of openness is usually erring on the side of grace.

More than anything else, it's fear of the costs of following Christ that keeps us stuck in place — that keeps individuals mired in moral mediocrity, that keeps families stagnantly safe and bourgeois, and that keeps the Church floundering in the mainstream instead of soaring on her proper transcendent plane. Families that are fulfilling their role as schools of grace will be *both* havens *and* beacons, providing moral and spiritual security for their members, especially children, while prudently offering others at least a glimpse of another way of being in the world.

This is what it means to conserve and to communicate the grace of regular participation in the sacraments and the grace of a regular prayer life. Grace is fertile, and not just in the sense of facilitating our participation in God's life-giving power through procreation. No, grace is "diffusive of itself," as the philosophers

The Prodigal Church

say: Because it is nothing less than God's divine life, it gives of itself, making more and more and more participation in divinity possible — unless we get in the way.

The family, at its best, acts as a diffuser of grace, both right now and through time. In the moment, the family distributes grace to extended relations and friends and neighbors and all who come in contact with it, from teachers to cashiers to panhandlers. Looking forward, the family distributes grace to the next generation, forming (God willing) myriad new Christians in fearless holiness, who then fan out into the world and into the future.

By demonstrating the diffusiveness of grace in its very being, the family, then, demonstrates to the world the transformative message of Jesus Christ not just for individual souls, but for society.

8

The Model Society

The Social Question

A renewed Church is one with a compelling vision for mankind transformed by grace. We saw this in the vision of the institutional Church's embracing her heavenly identity rather than her settling for worldly mediocrity. We saw this in the vision of the ministry and example of the saints, who are living icons of the power of grace. We saw this in the vision of the parish as the peace-filled home of the people of God and an example of a more beautiful, more real way of being in the world. And we saw this, just a moment ago, in the vision of the family as a school of grace.

All of these visions, however, fit the generally prescribed role of the Church in a liberal secular society: occupied with her own institutions and her own people, forming individuals and families in their spirituality. (Though the Church's place in the family is increasingly under threat, in part due to our own complacency, as we discussed last chapter.) But a genuinely, confidently renewed Church would not allow herself to be so hemmed in. The Church needs not just to articulate but to demonstrate that grace can heal, elevate, and perfect society just as surely as it can souls.

We can see this firstly in the Church's social teaching, which explodes the categories of "right-wing" versus "left-wing," "conservative" versus "liberal" that dominate our politics. The Church's thinking about our common life transcends our everyday (and clearly failing) politics. It's precisely for this reason that we need to boldly assert Catholic Social Teaching, as we discussed earlier. As we do this, however, we must remember that there's no strict separation between the Church's social teaching and her teaching on the nature and morality of sexuality, marriage, and family.

To this end, it's best not to think of the great documents on marriage and family of the last century—such as Pius XI's *Casti Connubii*,[39] St. Paul VI's *Humanae Vitae*, and St. John Paul II's *Familiaris Consortio*—as distinct from Catholic Social Teaching. They are, rather, integral parts of the social magisterium, articulating a vision of family life that implicitly, and often explicitly, has political, social, and economic prerequisites. Sometimes the crossover is very clear, as when, in *Casti Connubii*, Pius XI referred to Leo XIII's *Rerum Novarum*:

> And so, in the first place, every effort must be made to bring about that which Our predecessor Leo XIII, of happy memory, has already insisted upon, namely, that in the State such economic and social methods should be adopted as will enable every head of a family to earn as much as, according to his station in life, is necessary for himself, his wife, and for the rearing of his children, for "the laborer is worthy of his hire."[40] To deny this, or to make light of what is equitable,

[39] It's worth noting here that *Casti Connubii* reaffirmed Church teaching on artificial contraception in 1930, immediately after the Anglican Communion's disastrous capitulation at Lambeth. *Humanae Vitae*, though a document of incredible importance and vigor, didn't close a door that had been cracked open; it locked a door that had already been firmly shut.

[40] Luke 10:7.

is a grave injustice and is placed among the greatest sins by Holy Writ[41]; nor is it lawful to fix such a scanty wage as will be insufficient for the upkeep of the family in the circumstances in which it is placed. (117)

The confidently fruitful love that is built into the nature of humanity and the institution (and sacrament) of marriage implies duties not just to the married couple, but to the society they inhabit. An economic structure that makes childbearing disastrously costly relative to wages is anti-life and anti-marriage. It is an assault on the dignity of the person not just as a worker, but as a husband and father, or wife and mother. A society without ubiquitous artificial contraception would not look just the same as ours but with more babies: It would have to be radically reordered to ensure that economic and social circumstances could allow families to be confidently open to life.

The Church does herself no favors by talking about contraception as a "moral teaching" and economics as a "social teaching." Her teachings all hold together seamlessly—and quite beautifully, in fact, not just intellectually but in the way of living they envision. Every social teaching is a moral teaching, and every moral teaching, because men are social beings, is in some way a social teaching.

The reality of the Christian family, then, is relevant not just to the inner life of the family or even to the Church, but to every human society. The family is, after all, the foundation of every society.

First Things First

Scott Hahn wrote in his recent book on marriage and the social order, fittingly called *The First Society*, that marriage is the first society "in the order of time and of importance":

[41] Deut. 24:14–15.

The Prodigal Church

The consummation of the marriage is, in a real and radical way, a new beginning—the creation of a new family that is a reflection of the original creation of all humanity, except this time we participate *with* God. Whether or not God blesses the union with children, the couple has created something new that has never been before or will be again. This participation in God's creative power is the foundation of human society.

For this reason, the married couple is first not just in time but in importance. Without the uniquely creative power God has bestowed on that relationship, there can be no further community, no self-sustaining society. Therefore we must treat marriage with particular care and concern; we can say without disparaging other types of relationship that nothing has so much riding on it as marriage does. There is no substitute for the union of a man and woman as husband and wife.[42]

The family, founded on the natural reality of marriage, is both timeless and always new. It forms the conceptual and *human* foundation of every society while at the same time providing the engine of its continual renewal. Therefore the prevailing norms of family life become ingrained in society in a way no other kind of relationship or community can effect. Strong and stable families are essential (though not sufficient) for social solidarity; fragmented families seed cynicism and distrust in the very DNA[43] of society, making the common good difficult to discern and impossible to achieve.

Indeed, in the family—not just the nuclear household, but the extended clan—we see all of human society in microcosm. We see

---

[42] Scott Hahn, *The First Society: The Sacrament of Matrimony and the Restoration of the Social Order* (Steubenville: Emmaus Road Publishing, 2018), 17. Emphasis original.
[43] See ibid., 17–19, for expansion on this analogy.

the most enduring self-giving love (think of the Holy Family) and we see the most destructive hatred (think of Cain and Abel). We see the basics of politics, with siblings organizing their time and possessions and parents trying to impose something like order on the entire operation. We see the expansion of human connections through space and time, as the family fans out across regions and through generations.

Seen in this light, the family clearly is not and cannot be a purely private institution. While the family, beginning with the nuclear family and emanating outward to the extended family, has certain privileges that are proper to its nature — that is, parts of its inner life that should not be interfered with without grave reason[44] — its purpose is intrinsically public. It is less like a building block, static and self-contained, and more like a cell, participating dynamically in the life of the organism through communication not just of bits of information, but of aspects of its very self.

And thus it becomes clear that the Catholic vision of the family is necessarily a vision for all of society. A Church striding confidently into the middle part of the twenty-first century will not limit herself to the ostensibly private sphere, but will articulate what the increasingly confused and insecure people of our time want to hear: a bold and comprehensive vision of the good society. And the Catholic family is the proof of concept.

Solidarity is Possible

During the 2020 presidential campaign, Senator Bernie Sanders often used the rhetoric of solidarity. Here's a representative tweet during the primaries:

---

[44] This is the principle of subsidiarity articulated in Catholic Social Teaching.

If you have health insurance, I'm asking you to fight for
those who don't.
If you're native-born, I'm asking you to fight for the un-
documented.
If you can afford an education, I'm asking you to fight for
those who can't.
The only way we defeat Trump is with human solidarity.[45]

Now, setting aside the question of defeating the incumbent president, this is a pretty excellent description of solidarity. In fact,
without committing to any *particular* policy responses to the marginalized, the general concept could've been lifted more or less
directly from the teaching of any of the recent popes. Probably the
axiomatic definition of solidarity was set down by Pope St. John
Paul II in his encyclical *Sollicitudo Rei Socialis*:

> [Solidarity] is not a feeling of vague compassion or shallow
> distress at the misfortunes of so many people, both near and
> far. On the contrary, it is a firm and persevering determina-
> tion to commit oneself to the common good; that is to say
> to the good of all and of each individual, because we are all
> really responsible for all. This determination is based on the
> solid conviction that what is hindering full development is
> [the] desire for profit and [the] thirst for power. (38)

The problem with the senator's understanding of solidarity
isn't in his definition, but in his application thereof. By endors-
ing nearly limitless legal abortion, Sanders not only excludes the
most vulnerable human beings from his "solidarity," but severs the

---

[45] Bernie Sanders (@BernieSanders), Twitter, February 20, 2020,
2:38 p.m., https://twitter.com/BernieSanders/status/1230577609
261670400.

fundamental bond of intergenerational solidarity between mothers and their children. The result is a hollow and cruel facsimile of genuine solidarity.

Not much better—in some ways worse—is the denial of the possibility of solidarity at all. In response to Sanders's tweet, a popular congressman from Texas, Dan Crenshaw, placed "solidarity" in scare quotes and called the senator's vision "socialism." This kind of sneering at the idea of a robust common good reduces the possibilities of human community to precisely the "vague compassion or shallow distress" that John Paul II criticizes. The result isn't a society at all, but a collection of self-interested individuals out of which only the appearance of society emerges.

Our prevailing notions of politics and economics, therefore, exclude the genuine solidarity that is our calling and our happiness—our imperfect but real participation in the selfless communion that exists in heaven. A renewed Church will continue, through her institutions such as universities and charities and bishops' conferences, to participate in the nitty-gritty of making the present order more just and more bearable. But she won't stop with only prescribing bandages and palliatives; she will articulate a complete vision for what society can really be with the help of grace and the blinders of secular liberalism removed.

And she will do this because it is her right and duty to do so. Christ is not only King of Heaven and our hearts; He is the King of this world, too. While Christ's social kingship—especially the fact that all authority, including civil authority, comes from and is answerable to Him—is perhaps not as eschatologically important as His royal priesthood, it is particularly important to assert right now, because most people no longer believe in a principle that can unite diverse people in a shared dignity and a common purpose. Yes, this sounds fanciful to jaded modern ways of thinking, and no, I don't have a foolproof plan for bringing this social vision to fruition. But we do have proofs of concept in families who acknowledge Christ's place on His throne.

First, the family is the place where the virtues that make a broader solidarity possible are formed. It's where we learn to give our time and share our stuff without keeping a ledger of IOUs. It's where we learn that what Christopher Dawson called the "spirit of calculation" and I like to call the spirit of the quid pro quo, which insists that every good deed be compensated, is not just unnecessary but antithetical to communion and flourishing.[46] It's where we see that what John Paul II called a "civilization of love" is possible, at least in microcosm:

> Yet there is no true love without an awareness that God "is Love"—and that man is the only creature on earth which God has called into existence "for its own sake." Created in the image and likeness of God, man cannot fully "find himself" except through the sincere gift of self....
>
> The family is indeed—more than any other human reality—the place where an individual can exist "for himself" through the sincere gift of self. This is why it remains a social institution which neither can nor should be replaced: it is the "sanctuary of life."[47]

It is in giving of ourselves that we encounter and actualize the fullness of what we are meant to be: images of the God who gives of

---

[46] This is not to say that *commutative justice*, by which wrongs are redressed and promises enforced, is antisocial. Quite the opposite: It's essential to the common good. But when we think that every gift or kindness incurs a debt, the concepts of gift and kindness themselves—and thus the concept of genuine love—fall away.

[47] Pope St. John Paul II, letter to families *Gratissimam Sane* (February 2, 1994), nos. 13, 11.

Himself. And it is in the family, itself an image of the community of love that is the Holy Trinity, that this reality is not just manifested to the fullest, but propagated through society. The Christ-centered family lays the foundation of solidarity, then, both by forming the virtues of solidarity and by demonstrating their credibility to the surrounding world.

Perhaps most importantly, families defined by the spirit of self-giving demonstrate to the Church herself, especially to often jaded hierarchs and struggling laypeople, that the Catholic social vision is beautiful and achievable. So much of the dissipation of the Church's patrimony that has occurred is related to a crisis of confidence, a cynicism that goodness on Christ's terms is impossible and that His grace, contra 2 Corinthians 12:9, is insufficient. Joyful Catholic families provide a living counterexample, spurring the Church to a renewed boldness.

Part of that boldness is asserting the reality and efficacy of the sacraments as genuine means of participation in God's life, not as mere rites of passage. And the family points to the sacraments in a particular way, because the model society of the family doesn't emerge out of nowhere: It is founded on a particular relationship, that of husband and wife:

> When a man and woman in marriage mutually give and re-ceive each other in the unity of "one flesh," the logic of the sincere gift of self becomes a part of their life. Without this, marriage would be empty; whereas a communion of persons, built on this logic, becomes a communion of parents.[48]

And it is sacramental grace that makes this beautiful communion possible.

---

[48] Ibid., no. 11.

The Prodigal Church

The Sacraments

The relationship between marriage and the sacraments is built into the very nature of both — and it goes beyond simply the sacrament of matrimony. The concepts of marriage and sacrament are the two ways we can think about the mystical relationship between Christ and His Church: She is His Spouse, and she is the "sacrament of salvation":

> The saving work of his holy and sanctifying humanity is the sacrament of salvation, which is revealed and active in the Church's sacraments.... The seven sacraments are the signs and instruments by which the Holy Spirit spreads the grace of Christ the head throughout the Church which is his Body. The Church, then, both contains and communicates the invisible grace she signifies. It is in this analogical sense, that the Church is called a "sacrament."[49]

As we discussed regarding the parish, returning to a robust understanding of the reality and transformative power of the sacraments is essential to renewal. This is fundamentally because sacramental grace, and our cooperation with it, is *the* means by which the Church will be renewed. But this is also because our complacency about the sacraments is a primary barrier to that renewal.

Undercutting our witness to the beautiful necessity of God's sanctifying grace are two related ways in which we habitually think and speak about the sacraments. First, we often think of the sacraments as accessories to a well-lived life, as lovely rituals that give us meaning and peace, but whose value is ultimately subjective. Second, we tend to talk about the sacraments as just a "Catholic thing" — traditions that, like ancient ethnic festivals, have value

---

[49] *Catechism of the Catholic Church* (CCC), no. 774. See also *Lumen Gentium* no. 48.

for their participants, but are irrelevant to others, except as curiosities. Together, these ways of thinking reduce the sacraments to limited, subjective experiences whose value to the world has more to do with how they make us feel than with how they transform us and the world around us.

But the sacraments aren't effective only if we feel they are; by their very nature, they channel grace into our souls. And they heal and elevate and perfect us not as isolated individuals, but as members of communities, which, in turn, benefit and are transformed by grace. Finally, sacramental grace isn't essential to salvation only for those who think it is. The sacraments are for everyone in two ways: First, they are the ordinary means of salvation for everyone; second, the grace they channel to the world radiates outward to all of human civilization. And the deficit of this grace is obvious to all with eyes to see.

Now, I could continue to quote saints and popes and the *Catechism* about the genuine reality of the sacraments; about how we can be assured of participating in God's divine life (what a concept!) through them; about how the sacraments are the ordinary means by which we are given the grace to follow Christ and be raised to His glory. But the most precise theology in the world won't help most people come to understand and appreciate the real-life effects of sacramental grace. More than any other person or relationship or institution, it's marriage that demonstrates the reality and efficacy of the sacraments. The family is a fundamentally sacramental institution.

This begins, of course, with the sacrament of matrimony and its effect on the relationship between husband and wife. It is right here where the "civilization of love" is founded and propagated—but it is also where so much of the distrust and cynicism and brokenness of today's world comes from. By persevering in self-giving love even through the inevitable challenges of sharing life together, the sacramentally bound family demonstrates that matrimony isn't about throwing a big party or securing an obligatory document or fulfilling some ill-defined tradition, but about saying yes to God's offer of divine assistance in living out the marital covenant. By embracing the full communion of persons, including not just openness to life but an enduring and trusting vulnerability, the spouses demonstrate the reality of grace and its necessity—and thus the Church's necessity—to living beautifully.

Even the Church's own ministers too often treat matrimony as a box on a respectability checklist, with little or no concern for whether the couple are even attempting to live chastely. Their disinterest merely continues the cycle of sacramental complacency. If the institutional Church doesn't treat the sacrament seriously, neither will the spouses, and its efficacy will be limited. Boldly faithful Catholic families, however, challenge this despairing cynicism by showing what the sacrament really can do, if its grace is trusted and facilitated through prayer and docility to God's will. The Church through her ministry of grace elevates the family; the family, in turn, elevates the Church by extending that grace and witnessing to its transformative power.

In the last chapter we called the family the "school of grace." Here we can see that it is also the school of the sacraments. This begins with matrimony but continues through regular reception of Communion and confession. One of the best things parents can do is simply to make the sacraments part of everyday life, not extraordinary and mildly embarrassing incursions of religiosity. Parents do this by not just going to Mass and confession but discussing them casually with children. For those children, then, the sacraments of initiation must be seen as genuine initiations into new ways of being, with new privileges and new duties, not one-time rites of passage.

Doing it right shows first that *doing it right* is possible, then that *doing it right* is fruitful and beautiful. *Doing it right*, to be clear, doesn't refer to our own efforts independent of God, but rather our radical reliance on God, in the form of a devoted sacramental life. This doesn't mean that every such family will be candidates for magazine covers. The sacraments aren't magic; to believe they are is superstition. While faithfully approaching the sacraments is good in itself, it's not enough, and it doesn't excuse inattentiveness to virtue. And even when we really are growing in holiness, there will be incursions of doubt and sin, sometimes really harrowing ones. But the beauty of the sacramental family isn't in its pristineness, like that of a family preparing for an expensive photo shoot, but in its joy, its love, its endurance. In this way, the family becomes an amplifier of the grace of the sacraments.

Ministers of Grace

We think about parents in several ways: as providers, nurturers, disciplinarians, and so on. We rarely think of them as ministers, because that idea is too "religious"; and under secular liberalism only people whose business is religion, such as priests, are allowed to commit themselves fully to faith. But if the family is the model society, then religion has to be part of it; and for religion to be part of it, there need to be ministers.

As we've already discussed, the family is the domestic church. Churches need priests. While *ordained* ministers obviously have an irreplaceable role in the spiritual life of the family, the domestic church also needs its own kind of priests: the parents.

The "priesthood of all believers" into which we are initiated by baptism[50] tends to get misunderstood in one of two ways. On the one hand, most often, it's ignored entirely because we're so well trained by the prevailing order not to think of the laity as having

[50] CCC 1268.

genuine, comprehensive religious duties. On the other hand, some elevate it disproportionately, in order to deemphasize the priesthood of ordained, sacrificing priests of Jesus Christ. In between we find the quite lovely reality: that we all share in Christ's "prophetic and royal mission,"[51] that we are called not just to absorb His grace but to communicate it to others.

Laypeople generally actualize this aspect of our identity in Christ in the context of the domestic church: that is, as parents. Single people and couples without children fulfill this priestly role in using their enhanced freedom to minister to each other, to families, to the poor, and so on, in genuine friendship. (More on this in the next chapters.) But parents have a special priestly responsibility toward their children; while this falls in a particular way on the father, who represents God and the pastor through his special authority, it is absolutely a shared calling.

The families where the sacraments are everyday parts of life, where communal prayer is a given, and where this duty of priestly ministry is taken up by parents and communicated to children: These are the families from which vocations to the priesthood and religious life will disproportionately arise. And this is precisely because these families will model the *completeness* of human society, with our "vertical" religious duties to God married to our "horizontal" duties to our fellow men. When you add the vertical to the horizontal, you get the cruciform reality of the family, of society, of life.

Out of the cruciform will emerge men and women who will be open to embracing the cross in the form of religious life. After all, despite our bloodless secularism, priests and monks and nuns are essential to a complete society. The sacramental ministry of the priest channels the grace that makes society possible at all,

[51] Ibid.

and the perpetual prayers of vowed religious are more important to civilization than a million management consultants. Families that embrace the complete reality of the spiritual life, including the ministerial role of the parents, will produce children who desire to take on any of the roles in a genuinely complete society—that is, one that's ordered first to God, not prosperity or autonomy or some other idol.

In other words, considering the priesthood or religious life should be *normal*, like considering being a doctor, plumber, or firefighter. It's part of the family's role in laying out the contours of reality, which we discussed last chapter, and thereby *creating* that reality for itself and those around it. Treating the priesthood as the socially and spiritually essential vocation that it is: That's how you get more priests.

To this end, there's no substitute for spending time with your parish priests and, as much as possible, with other priests and religious. When the priest is just the man who celebrates weekly Mass at a distance, it's much harder for a boy to imagine filling that role—especially if all the talk in the home is about someday choosing a "regular" occupation. So make priests normal. Insist that your pastor come over for dinner; go to parish functions and shoot the breeze with him; invite him to your baptism reception; make him a regular part of life, because he *is* a regular part of life—of your spiritual good and of the common good of your family and community.

One of the most admirable traits in a priest is the ability to be affable without sacrificing the gravitas of his office. It makes a tremendous impression on children to see men of God who are both unmistakably noble and completely at ease in family life. In places with priest shortages this kind of intimacy will get harder as priests become busier, but it's all the more important as priests become lonelier, too.

The Prodigal Church

And so the grace-filled ministry of parenting is fruitful, because grace is always fruitful. It forms a genuine society in miniature and nurtures in the next generation a love of priestly ministry, whether the priesthood of the baptized or the priesthood of the altar. And it strengthens our resolve to go out boldly and fulfill Christ's "prophetic and royal mission."

We're All Missionaries

The language of the conflict between Christian civilization and liberal secular civilization is usually martial: culture wars and rhetorical battlefields and so on. The Catholic family even gets drafted into the fight as a training ground in the demographic struggle, as we look to take advantage of secularists' peculiar disinterest in reproduction.

Of course martial imagery is far from unknown in Scripture. I always think of that wonderful passage in Ephesians:

> Therefore take the whole armor of God, that you may be able to withstand in the evil day, and having done all, to stand. Stand therefore, having girded your loins with truth, and having put on the breastplate of righteousness, and having shod your feet with the equipment of the gospel of peace; above all taking the shield of faith, with which you can quench all the flaming darts of the evil one. And take the helmet of salvation, and the sword of the Spirit, which is the word of God. Pray at all times in the Spirit, with all prayer and supplication. (Eph. 6:13–18)

You'll notice, though, that while the imagery is that of the soldier, the spirit is that of the missionary. The warrior for Christ is a person of truth, righteousness, faith, prayer, and *peace*. And the fact of the matter is that the view from just about any front porch in America is not of a cultural battleground—that was the previous war, and we were routed—but a mission field. The battle is not against a human enemy but the devil, and the prize is not influence but souls. The family is at the front lines, but resembles more closely the Jesuits who fanned across the Americas to evangelize the indigenous than the soldiers in the trenches of the Great War. The family is like a base community rather than a barracks.

In *The Mission*, another luminous reading from St. Paul catalyzes Robert de Niro's character's transformation from mercenary slaver to Jesuit missionary:

> If I speak in the tongues of men and of angels, but have not love, I am a noisy gong or a clanging cymbal. And if I have prophetic powers, and understand all mysteries and all knowledge, and if I have all faith, so as to remove mountains, but have not love, I am nothing. If I give away all I have, and if I deliver my body to be burned, but have not love, I gain nothing....
>
> When I was a child, I spoke like a child, I thought like a child, I reasoned like a child; when I became a man, I gave up childish ways.... So faith, hope, love abide, these three; but the greatest of these is love. (1 Cor. 13:1–3, 11, 13)

The family is the soil of love, of prayer, of peace out of which missionary fortitude can grow and thrive. And this does require fortitude: We are surrounded by nearly unprecedented spiritual poverty and despair. The words of Pope Francis about evangelizing the poor of the Amazon apply just as well to the needs of contemporary America:

> An authentic option for the poor and the abandoned, while motivating us to liberate them from material poverty and to defend their rights, also involves inviting them to a friendship

with the Lord that can elevate and dignify them. How sad it would be if they were to receive from us a body of teachings or a moral code, but not the great message of salvation, the missionary appeal that speaks to the heart and gives meaning to everything else in life. Nor can we be content with a social message. If we devote our lives to their service, to working for the justice and dignity that they deserve, we cannot conceal the fact that we do so because we see Christ in them and because we acknowledge the immense dignity that they have received from God, the Father who loves them with boundless love.[52]

This is a description of the authentic, comprehensive Christian message: social *and* moral, law *and* friendship, all ordered toward salvation in Christ—"the great message of salvation … that speaks to the heart and gives meaning to everything else in life." We might not have a crisis of political and economic oppression—at least not as severely—as does the Amazon, but we do have a crisis of cynicism, of despair, of meaninglessness. And it's almost all related not to the lack of material well-being, but to obsession with it.

The family is the lynchpin of a truly missionary, energetic Church for the twenty-first century. It demonstrates what a community of persons can be through grace—self-giving, vulnerable, trusting, peaceful—and then produces the very people who can go out into the world with that message of love and salvation.

Every family, though, is embedded in a community that should support and extend its mission of grace. These communities, forged by friendship, will be catalysts and capstones of renewal.

---

[52] Pope Francis, post-synodal apostolic exhortation *Querida Amazonia* (February 2, 2020), no. 63.

Part 5

Friendship and Community

9

The Foundation

Ethnogenesis

Thus far we have slowly zoomed the camera in, from the universal Church to the local Church to the domestic Church. The natural next step, I suppose, is the temple of the Holy Spirit that is the individual. The renewal of the Church undoubtedly depends on the renewal of each of her members. But rather than focusing on individual spiritual growth — the teachings of the saints, the masters of holiness, have you covered — I'll stay in my lane and keep the focus on what we can do *together*.

In any event, one of the running themes of this book is that there's no strict demarcation between the individual and the communal, between the private and the public. Condoning off the individual has been one of liberal secularism's most effective techniques for dulling our sense of duty to our fellow men, to the Church, and to God. And so, while deepening one's relationship with Christ, His Mother, and His saints is absolutely essential, personal sanctity is both manifested and strengthened in relationship with others. It all rises and falls together.

Because of the interconnectedness of the life of faith, its ecological dynamism and complexity, we can't possibly identify a single foundation for renewal. Of course we can say, and will continue to

The Prodigal Church

say, that everything depends on God's grace, and our responsiveness to it. This entire book is about drawing out the implications of that truth for our institutions and relationships. And we can emphasize that every level of the Church, from the universal to the particular, builds on that grace in its own proper way.

There's something missing, though—something that I think can genuinely be called *the foundation* for renewal, especially in the twenty-first century: the revitalization of authentic Christian community. This is about more than the family, the parish, and the institutional Church; it's about rediscovering not just that the Church is the people of God in an abstract sense, but that she really constitutes *a people*, one more real than any national or ethnic or political group. The identity we share with our fellow Catholics in Christ and in the sacraments isn't just a sharing in history or ritual or tradition; it's a sharing in divine life, *together*, right now.

Social scientists call the process by which a group comes to consciousness of its own distinctness as a community "ethnogenesis"—literally, "the beginning or creation of a people." It's a politically and culturally loaded term, implicating difficult questions about how *real* ethnic and racial groups actually are, how much the distinctions among them are socially and politically constructed, and whether new ones can form at all. Luckily we don't have to worry about all that: As adopted sons and daughters of God, baptized and confirmed Catholics are *objectively* different because our souls have been indelibly marked by His grace.[53]

---

[53] All Christians who are baptized with the trinitarian formula are also brought into God's family, and so we share something transcendent with them. The complete initiation of Communion and confirmation, though, brings a person more fully into the bosom of the Church: Confirmation "completes" baptism and "imprints on the soul an *indelible spiritual mark*, ... which is the sign that Jesus Christ has marked a Christian with the seal of his Spirit by clothing

The problem is that we don't act like it. Too often we identify as "Catholic" as if it were a brand name, while allowing our political and national and ethnic identities, rather than our identity in Christ, to shape our lives. Indeed, the idea that we might have special responsibilities to our fellow Catholics, that we might treat them in any way differently from anyone else, prompts a nearly allergic reaction in the modern American mind. All kinds of nasty-sounding words leap into our heads: "intolerant," "prejudiced," "discriminatory."

Let's home in on that last one: discriminatory. To discriminate means to treat different things, well, differently. To discriminate is not inherently bad; we can see this in the term "discriminating." A person has discriminating taste if he recognizes and treats different types of food, music, and so on according to their quality. It is not unjust or prejudicial to savor a well-prepared duck breast more than a microwaved chicken nugget, or a baroque concerto more than a modernist cacophony; it is, in fact, good—a sign of applying reason to the experiences of our senses.

Our negative association with the idea of discrimination comes from the ubiquity of *unjust* discrimination in our history and present. The problem with, for instance, treating black and white Americans differently under the law is that whatever ways they differ have *no relevance whatsoever* to their equal dignity, which is the basis of equality under the law. Treating differently things that are not actually different in relevant ways is irrational, and gravely unjust when applied to human society. Treating people of different colors differently in terms of *skincare regimes*, on the other hand, is perfectly reasonable and just discrimination; it recognizes that the differences are relevant in a limited way in this area. We just aren't accustomed to hearing the word used in this way.

---

him with power from on high so that he may be his witness" (CCC 1304, emphasis original).

The Prodigal Church

And so, yes, Catholic ethnogenesis would involve a certain amount of personal discrimination — but *reasonable and just* discrimination based on *real and relevant* differences. This doesn't mean denying non-Catholics any of the responsibilities of love and kindness and hospitality and charity that we owe to every person; that *would* be unjust. But it does mean giving pride of place in our lives to those with whom we share not just a Faith but a filial relationship with God the Father and full membership in the Church of Jesus Christ. It means intentionally forming the friendships, which in turn form the communities, that will make it more realistic to follow Christ on the journey of renewal.

St. Peter put it as concisely as possible: "Honor all men. Love the brotherhood" (1 Pet. 2:17). We don't overlook any man, woman, or child; we don't scowl or contemn or condescend. Part of being marked by baptism is being called to a higher dignity, but that dignity manifests itself not in haughtiness but in humility and service to all.

That calling, however, is also to membership in an objectively distinct community of persons. We have forgotten this, as we've been catechized by the liberal doctrine of not just *equality* but *homogeneity*. We have been folded into secular society and have internalized the notion that whatever is distinctive about our Faith must be expressed only individually; communal religious services are fine, but *religious communities* are frightening and intolerant and closed-minded and, worst of all, illiberal. Yes, a few oddities have been grandfathered in, such as various Anabaptist sects, but they are anachronisms — living museum pieces worthy of gawking more than imitation.

In other words, the dissipation of doctrine and tradition and culture has been paralleled by a dissipation of persons. In public we are to conduct ourselves as undifferentiated members of mass society, participating in the same pastimes and aspirations and blasphemies as everybody else, as if there were no God or Church or sacraments. Outside our homes and churches there are to be no Christians or Jews or Muslims but only good seculars[54]; even though American culture broadly remains more religious than most Western nations, the lowest common denominator is still casual atheism. And we have acquiesced, compromising Christian authenticity for membership in the herd.

This is particularly upsetting when we see that other groups with a far less transcendent distinctiveness have been allowed to form communities of solidarity. For decades, for instance, members of what we now call the LGBT community have intentionally formed friendships and clubs and associations and entire neighborhoods to protect themselves from a hostile culture and to nurture their perceived particularity. Interestingly, the welcoming of this community into the mainstream has similarly resulted in its dissipation, with a great deal of tension between those thrilled to have "made it" and those worried about losing the solidarity that made their communities vibrant and powerful. But even today it is still common for members of the community to seek one another out, before others, for friendship and support.

If this community can do it, why can't we? What we share—the Body and Blood of Jesus Christ—is much deeper and more important and more *real* than what an alliance of sexual minorities shares. We shouldn't feel uncomfortable about seeking out fellow Catholics for friendship primarily on the basis of their Catholicism, or about feeling especially warm toward a new acquaintance when we realize he's Catholic. This isn't unjust discrimination; it's a recognition of reality.

---

[54] This is taken to the extreme in the principle of *laïcité* in France, which has resulted in outright legal prohibitions on religious dress or even accessories in public. The pressure in the United States is thankfully more social than legal—but still absolutely real.

The Prodigal Church

Friends Forever

Friendship makes this spiritual reality a social reality. Friendship too often gets overlooked in Catholic discourse, but it's absolutely essential to understanding the proper relationship among members of the Body of Christ, and between us and Christ. We talk as if romantic love is the apex of human sociality, and the only kind of love worthy of serious attention. While friendship, unlike romantic love, is not ordered toward a *complete* communion of persons, bodily and spiritually, friendship is not inferior or inessential.

This casual approach to friendship is both reflected in and reinforced by the way we practice it. We treat friendships as arbitrary and temporary, as side effects of our other duties. When work calls us to another city or our children transfer to another school, our relationships change, with some being terminated, or at least downgraded, while new friendships of convenience form. We experience friendship passively, as something that happens to us rather than something we choose and participate in and work at. And so the idea that friendships might involve *love* sounds strange—too intimate, too permanent, too intense. Yet Jesus uses the language of friendship to deliver one of His most beautiful discourses on love:

> This is my commandment, that you love one another as I have loved you. Greater love has no man than this, that a man lay down his life for his friends. You are my friends if you do what I command you. No longer do I call you servants, for the servant does not know what his master is doing; but I have called you friends, for all that I have heard from my Father I have made known to you. You did not choose me, but I chose you and appointed you that you should go and bear fruit and that your fruit should abide; so that whatever you ask the Father in my name, he may give it to you. This I command you, to love one another. (John 15:12–17)

Not only is self-sacrificial friendship not inferior to romantic love; it is the greatest love. It is the love that Christ Himself manifested in His Passion. It is the love we are called to have for Him in return—the desire and the will to give up anything, including our very lives, for Him. Friendship is the relationship Christ had with His apostles, and has with us when we follow Him. It is, in turn, the way He calls us to relate to our fellow members of His Body.

If marriage is the skeleton key for understanding the relationship between Christ and the Church, and if the family is the skeleton key for understanding the relationship between the faithful and God the Father and Holy Mother Church, then friendship is the skeleton key for understanding the relationship among the faithful. Friendship is, uniquely, the form of intimacy demonstrated for us by Christ during His earthly ministry; while His status as Son and Bridegroom is mystical, His status as friend was and is corporeal.

Indeed, we revitalize this sacrificial friendship at every Mass and every Communion. We are transported to the foot of the Cross, where Christ showed us what love really asks of us. We are united with Him sacramentally, which includes spiritually and bodily—which does not mean, of course, sexually, but in an act of sacrifice and mercy. Then we are to go out and spread the grace of that sacrifice to the world—but in a particular way to our fellow members of His Body.

"Love one another *as I have loved you*." We take the love He offers us and reflect it to others. One of the greatest fruits of the Mass, and of all the sacraments, is genuine friendship.

The Sacramentality of Friendship

The sacraments exemplify the deep corporeality of the Catholic Faith. One of the most scandalous aspects of the young Christian Church to pagan Romans was the notion that God would become man. For the Romans, this was a category error, like saying a noble pine tree decided one day to become a mushroom. Even if it were possible, no *reasonable* deity would give up all the perks of godliness to muck around among us. And so they thought the Christians were both blasphemous and nuts.

The Romans were right, of course, that the self-emptying, self-sacrificing Deity is scandalous in human terms. As St. Paul wrote, "We preach Christ crucified, a stumbling block to Jews and *folly to Gentiles*" (1 Cor. 1:23, emphasis added). And the personal, embodied duties of service that this new incarnational religion demanded were scandalous to a utilitarian and materialist culture. That's exactly, of course, why the early Christians leaned into the scandal of service and sacrifice and sacrament, accentuating the contradictions with pagan norms and expectations. The Christian truth of embodied service and spirituality, it turns out, accords with our own dual nature—the nature God gave us—as body and spirit. And so the scandalized Romans were routed by love and truth. As St. Paul concluded, "For the foolishness of God is wiser than men, and the weakness of God is stronger than men" (1 Cor. 1:25).

Incidentally, it's the removal or denial of corporeality that is at the heart of so many Protestant errors. Whitewashed churches, spare liturgies, minimized (or eliminated) sacraments, discarded feasts and fasts—these are all ostensibly about forming a "purer," less encumbered faith. But they cut against the embodied reality of the God we worship, which is reflected in our own embodied nature. The loving communion we are called to have with Him and our fellow men is comprehensive: It involves the body and the soul.

Christian friendship is a reflection of the Incarnation just as the sacraments are. Of course, bringing a meal to a postpartum mother, grasping the shoulder of a struggling father, or attending the funeral of a friend's relative is not numbered among the seven sacraments, but each is an act of trust and service that involves the body and the soul. And, like the sacraments, these acts communicate grace.

One of the most important qualities of grace is that it is communicable; that is, it can be spread from person to person through acts of love. This makes sense: If grace is participation in God's divine life, then of course it is inexhaustible, desiring to bring all things to perfection. Furthermore, by allowing grace to conform us to Christ, we share that divine life quite literally by *being Christ* to and for others. Grace is like a very good, very contagious virus—but it's also much more: It transforms us into its source, Jesus Christ.

And so friendship is both an expression of grace—an expression of what it means to be transformed into the Messiah who calls us friends—and a means by which grace is propagated into the world. It is the premier participation, outside of divine worship and the sacraments themselves, in the divine life of Christ mediated through the Church. It extends the saving work of sacramental grace beyond the four walls of the church building and beyond ourselves, bringing that grace to a more complete fruition than if we tried vainly and timidly to hoard it.

Friendship is sacramental, then, in at least three ways. First, it communicates grace. Second, it involves service of and to both the body and the soul. And third, it is commanded by Christ.

We can see, then, that friendship is not optional. If grace is the foundation of all community in the spiritual realm, friendship, as the activation and propagation of that grace, is its foundation in the social realm. Communities don't appear out of nowhere, nor are they formed by simple consent and contract; they begin, especially in a time of alienation like our own, with the choice to be friends.

Choosing Friendship

I remember the first time I realized I had grown-up friends. I had (a few) middle school friends, and some high school friends, and some really wonderful college friends, but after I moved back home to

The Prodigal Church

Pittsburgh, they were all out of the picture. I had my fiancée (she counts for something!) and my parents, with whom I lived for a year or so until my wedding, but that was that.

Now that we have four children and many very close friends — more on that soon — it's hard for me to remember what that time in my life was like. I was very busy working in politics, which for better or worse mitigated the loneliness. I don't really know what I thought the future held — maybe a growing collection of work colleagues and political acquaintances who passed for friends? In the meantime, my wife and I would go to our parish's young adult ministry events, which involved a short spiritual talk and then hanging out at a local bar.

We met one couple there who were just dating at the time, and who seemed especially keen on including us in their lives. They invited us to things like gingerbread-house-making nights and board game nights at the young woman's somewhat dingy apartment. It was very basic stuff, but I wasn't used to being comfortable in another person's home; more precisely, I wasn't used to others' being comfortable with me, or any company for that matter, in their less than immaculate homes — other than college dorms. It was an invitation to friendship and a little example of vulnerability and trust, the kind of grace-filled choice that bears fruit.

We ended up becoming quite close with this couple; they now live half a block from us and we're godparents to one of each other's children. But before all that happened, my wife and I met some more young Catholics and moved twice and had two children. Our new home was in a neighborhood with some of these acquaintances, which was a nice bonus, but I wasn't yet sure it would amount to anything.

I realized that it was amounting to something when one day I came home from a dinner event expecting to find my wife and two children quietly puttering about. Instead, when I opened the door I was nearly knocked over with the din of multiple families with several children in my living room. My wife had thrown an impromptu taco party in my absence. But instead of being taken aback, I immediately integrated into the party, greeted other parents' children, participated in witty chitchat with fellow dads, and, simply, felt completely at home. I realized that I hadn't felt this comfortable with people, especially in *my space*, since the special relationships of my college days. I finally had real friends again.

That's the summary version of what could be a long story. I focused on that first couple from the young adult ministry events, but I could have chosen other anecdotes about other families. In so many cases, the beginning and the nurturing of friendship were about simply extending or accepting an invitation to be with other people. It's about saying yes to the people God has placed in our lives, which is part of saying yes to God. Then it's about extending that yes by *choosing* to go a little deeper into vulnerability and its counterpart, trust. It won't happen on its own.

Choosing friendship entails choosing vulnerability, because the only way to grow in communion with others is to let people into our imperfect lives. Vulnerability and trust are in a catch-22 relationship: In order to grow in trust, we must make ourselves vulnerable; but in order to feel comfortable making ourselves vulnerable, we have to trust that we won't be hurt. Someone has to make the first move. Grace makes that leap of faith possible, and is communicated to others in the process.

This is why unfussy domestic hospitality is so important to growing in friendship: Letting others into our messy homes is a small step toward letting them into our messy souls. The leap of faith to allow others to see our sour milk spills and diaper box décor and laundry explosions gives our guests permission to do the same for someone else. The chain of hospitality is a chain of grace, made possible by an initial choice to be vulnerable.

The Prodigal Church

Indeed, one of the clearest symptoms of our culture's spurning of grace is our horror of vulnerability. It's important to say here that not all fears are illegitimate or faithless: We live in a fallen world, seemingly falling further every day, and exploitation of vulnerability is real and potentially devastating. Vulnerability requires prudence. In the same way that we wouldn't give a new plumber a tour of our bedroom, we shouldn't expose the tenderest parts of our soul to every seemingly friendly person at a party.

But our culture's aversion to vulnerability goes well beyond prudence. We struggle to let others into our lives because we fear they won't like what they see—and when we lack confidence in God's everlasting love, their rejection feels like a rejection of our very dignity and personhood. And because, as a culture, we've rejected God's healing grace, we don't believe our souls can ever be made whole again. And so we're left nursing interior wounds we refuse to expose to anyone who can help, all while masking our pain with often pathetic attempts at perfection. The result, often enough, is crippling loneliness and self-doubt—*especially* among those who appear most social and successful.

Only the grace of vulnerability can break the cycle. This is why *choosing* friendship, not just letting it happen, is among the most radical acts in today's world.

Nuclear Option

One of the most beautiful fruits of friendship is also among the hardest to admit we need: sharing the burdens of everyday life. The American creed of self-sufficiency interacts with the modern obsession with autonomy—and not to mention regular old pride—to create a strong incentive never to admit we need anyone for anything. One of the most difficult acts of vulnerability in friendship, one usually downstream from hospitality, is asking for help.

Again, this aspect of genuine friendship reflects our relationship with Christ. Our insufficiency in the material realm — that is, our dependence on others to survive, let alone thrive — is analogous to our insufficiency in the spiritual realm — our inability to save our own souls. Getting up the gumption explicitly to rely on others helps us to admit that we also rely on Christ for everything good. And it works the other way, too: A robust prayer and sacramental life prepares us to participate humbly in an interdependent community.

Autonomy and self-sufficiency are thought to be the preconditions of liberty, but nothing could be further from the truth. The isolated person is uninsulated against instability, both external and internal. Externally, he is much more easily buffeted by changing winds at work or in the broader economy or among his social circles. Internally, he is more at the mercy of his state of mind, his emotions, and his desires. Altogether, he is not independent but *completely dependent* on realities beyond his control, all while insisting to the contrary.

Genuine friendships, while often perceived as constraining, are in fact liberating. It doesn't take that many friends to form a network of material and social and spiritual support, with each member's shortcomings compensated by another's strengths. Sometimes it's unsettling to talk with someone who is clearly more advanced in some aspect of sanctity or parenting or home improvement, but these are opportunities for learning and growth. Moreover, habits of candid conversation about our weaknesses become habits of humility that propagate through the network: Everyone is learning from and helping everybody else, growing in trust and generosity all the time. Whether you realize it or not, there's *something* about you that others admire and learn from.

The mutual sharing of wisdom and know-how and service leaves everyone freer to follow God's will for his life. Liberated from at least

The Prodigal Church

some of our limitations, either through learning from or leaning on our friends, we can more confidently put our God-given talents to use in this world, while dedicating more time and energy to the spiritual life. In my own family, I credit our friends' example and teaching with everything from inspiring our daily family Rosary to the confidence to take on home improvement projects that I would have balked at only a year or two ago. And I like to think that, maybe, from time to time, I drop a *bon mot* that helps somebody in some way.

Nothing could be clearer, from both the theory and the practice of this kind of friendship, than the insufficiency of the insulated nuclear family as the model of Catholic community. In its proper way, as we've discussed at length, the household of parents and their children is essential to passing on the Faith and forming a generation primed for renewal. More than that, the nuclear family has pride of place in the Christian imagination because the Messiah was born into and raised within such a household. But from the time of Christ (and long before) until very recently, the nuclear household was not expected to be isolated or self-sufficient.

In our age of atomization, it's tempting to look to the nuclear family as a step toward rediscovering the communal. But historically it worked in the other direction: The emerging dominance of the nuclear family during the twentieth century was part of the process of social fragmentation. The retreat of the nuclear household behind its suburban picket fence wasn't the preservation of a communal ethic, but a key factor in its destruction. Thus to let the nuclear family dominate the Catholic social imagination isn't to strike a blow against individualism at all, but to acquiesce to it. Rather, the prime social condition for a renewed Church will be an archipelago of robust Catholic communities, not isolated Catholic families.

The Foundation

Catalyzing Community

Habits of vulnerability and trust, habits of hospitality, habits of service: It doesn't take too many friendships built on these, especially in reasonably close proximity, to form a real community. These sacramental friendships lay the fertile soil of grace from which a community based in love and sacrifice and service, not calculation and contract and quid pro quos, can emerge and thrive.

This all might sound a little too good to be true, a little naïve, a little utopian. Of course there will be stumbling blocks in every friendship, and especially in networks of friendships: We can't outrun our brokenness forever. Part of growing in virtue together is growing in the prudence to know when things are going askew. Part of growing in trust is building up the goodwill to respond compassionately when someone breaks that trust. But even with all the virtue in the world, sin finds a way.

I can't express enough, though, how much I dislike the notion that any community beyond the family is bound to fail spectacularly. This is despair of the power of grace, plain and simple. It's the same hopeless, faithless thinking that leads secular members of my generation to eschew marriage out of fear of divorce. If grace isn't real and powerful, then this is a perfectly reasonable way to think. But if it is real, then wallowing in fear when we're called to live boldly as signs of Christian contradiction is practical atheism.

And forming those liberating, grace-reinforced friendships, which become the sinews that give strength and structure to emergent communities, is one of the most strikingly contradictory tasks we can undertake in our age of cynical individualism. It's how we demonstrate to the world, to our fellow Catholics, and to ourselves that God's participation in our lives isn't abstract but constructive and beautiful. After all, if friendship is possible — and it must be, because Christ called us to it directly — then so is this kind of robust community.

The Prodigal Church

To be clear, I'm not talking about taking over a town on the Dakota prairie or clearing out a commune within a national forest or even forming some kind of bespoke urban parish. What I'm talking about is *organic*, the natural result of intentional friendship-formation, and will look entirely different with different people in different contexts. It's not about desperately fitting a particular model, but about letting the fertile grace of friendship simply *work* as God intends it to in our lives.

In my case, young families are being drawn to an emerging community in a middle-class city neighborhood by the appeal of living close to fellow Catholics in a similar stage of life. In other cases, it may be a particular parish or other institution that exerts a gravitational pull; in others still, a higher degree of intentionality, such as a common commitment to a particular way of living or to redressing a particular injustice, may prevail. The possibilities are endless, and this is another beautiful attribute of grace: the infinite variety of its applications, even while it always directs us back to its one Source.

What these communities will all share is their distinctive Catholicity. They will be, if they are to survive, founded on the sacraments, energized by prayer for and with one another, and constantly nourished by service. And out of them will emerge the virtues and the confidence that make Church renewal possible. They will demonstrate that the ministry of the Church enables the kind of transparently beautiful communion that we're told is impractical or impossible. Thus they will be attractive symbols of hope to a fragmented, uprooted civilization. But more than that, they will show the members of the communities themselves, especially children, that comprehensive Catholic identity, tradition, and practice are worth living—and dying—for.

10

The Keystone

A Vision

The institutional Church, the parish, and the family are all essential to the flourishing of the Body of Christ here on earth. But it's friendship and community that will knit the people of God together in the twenty-first century.

It's not about re-creating the urban Catholic ghettoes of the early twentieth century, or the thriving parishes of midcentury, or the mediocre status quo ante the sex abuse crisis. It's not about mimicking other emergent religious communities or megachurches or social-service nonprofits. It's not about doing what's expected of us in any sense the secular world would recognize.

It is about something more radical: grace, virtue, communion, salvation. It is about applying the Church's patrimony — in teaching and culture and tradition — to the conditions of today, emphasizing that which is most contradictory to the increasingly distrusted and mistrustful spirit of the age. It is about holiness at all costs, lived together.

It's in Catholic communities of friendship that the costs of holiness become more readily bearable. First, there's the example of others, which builds up into community norms of sacrifice for Christ, for justice, and for each other. Then, there's the confidence that comes with that sacrifice, the sure knowledge that we will be lifted up spiritually, emotionally, socially, and materially when the costs rise or misfortune strikes. Finally, there's the fertile foundation of prayer, a strong and resilient matrix of divine life, each person supporting the others, all tethered to the Holy Spirit and Holy Mother Church.

I imagine these communities appearing seemingly spontaneously as individual Catholics or Catholic families seek stability and security in an increasingly alienated and confused civilization. Living in physical and spiritual proximity—that is, regularly sharing everyday life, prayer, and liturgical worship—will continue to shift from being a luxury for the fortunate to a necessity for anyone who desires to follow Christ to the fullest in what is shaping up to be a long and tumultuous twenty-first century.

Sometimes, as we've said, these communities will coalesce around an already existing parish; other times, though, it will be a job center, or a neighborhood with the right mix of housing stock and price point, or an institution like a Catholic Worker house—wherever gravity begins to build up. Like space rocks that merge and exert a greater and greater pull as they combine, this coalescence will rarely be predictable or respect existing boundaries and bureaucratic distinctions. It'll be important, then, for parishes and dioceses to foster these communities on their own terms, not by trying to shoehorn them into existing structures.

This might mean offering a priest as a kind of very part-time chaplain, or scheduling events specifically for the community even if its members don't all belong to the same parish. In our growing neighborhood of Catholic families, for instance, the neighborhood parish hosts a Bible study *with childcare*—not a small undertaking given the reams of clearances and background checks needed these days—even though most of the families who participate belong to the Latin-Mass parish across town. This warm openness allows spiritual cross-pollination and enhances the unity of the people of God. Over time, as these communities grow, dioceses may even consider redrawing parish lines or establishing personal parishes to respond to the new distribution of the faithful. The Catholic geography of 2050 will be radically different from that of 1950, and the structure of the Church should reflect that.

There won't always be homogeneity of spirituality or liturgical preference in these communities, and that's fine: Catholicity includes and enhances genuine diversity.[55] But there should be a common commitment to prayer and not just tolerance to other views but openness to experiencing other forms of worship. Among our friends, several attend a Latin-Mass parish, some go to Eastern-Rite parishes, and some are committed to reviving the established neighborhood parish, whose future is in doubt due to consolidation. While there would be a certain blessing to having everyone in the same liturgical community, there's also a blessing to letting each family discern its calling, knowing that others will support not just its decision but its mission.

I imagine having one, or a few, or several of these communities in every city, and many in towns and all over the countryside—a nationwide archipelago of grace and security and distinctive, attractive, authentic Catholic identity. Just as each member of these communities

---

[55] This raises the question of racial and ethnic diversity. It's pious optimism that the diversity of these communities will naturally converge with that of the surrounding Catholic population. In practice, though, parishes are often already de facto segregated, with historically Black and Latino parishes remaining so, suburban parishes remaining lily white, and mixed-language parishes having parallel ministries that rarely meet. I don't have a good solution for this—it's a social-structural problem—other than to say that emerging Catholic communities should be cognizant of it and thus intentionally inclusive of Catholics of color, non-English speakers (perhaps learning Spanish could be part of homeschool curricula), immigrants, and so on. This is part of the calling to *justice* that every Catholic shares, and that robust communities enhance.

feels welcome in the home of any other member, so would out-of-town Catholic visitors be assured of hospitality in any community. I've lost count of the number of guests we and our friends have hosted; on one occasion, due to a scheduling conflict, at the last minute we put up our own college friends in someone else's house. They stayed up well past midnight talking about their shared Faith, the greatest unifier of all, and they still swap Christmas cards every year.

This is a vision of the Body of Christ in the twenty-first century. It doesn't overturn the structures and traditions of the past, but applies them in creative ways to new circumstances. It also doesn't displace those who have been reasonably well served by the status quo; it's not about destroying but augmenting, providing an option for a way of living that many desire but few think is possible or practical. It's more adaptive reuse than creative destruction.

The truth is that the way things are—largely isolated households popping into Mass weekly then going their own ways, back into the world on their own terms—is not sustainable. This way of living is simply no match for the corrosive power of individualism, liberal secularism, and consumer capitalism. Renewal will only come with a renewed confidence in the radicalism of Christ's message of love, peace, justice, and salvation. This confidence will, in turn, rise and fall with a renewed way of living in the world.

After Individualism

It would be one thing to suggest this when the present order seemed to be strong and stable, fulfilling the material and spiritual needs of the people who make up American civilization. If things seemed to be going well across the board, you might object that this vision of community is *nice*, and maybe even rooted in some real truth, but neither essential nor terribly appealing when the prevailing way of living is serving people well.

First of all, this is exactly the complacency that resulted in the dissipation of Catholic heritage. We became so comfortable, so tamed, in an increasingly God-denying culture that we didn't even notice what was happening — not just the passing away of our identity and tradition but their replacement by secular simulacra. Even more important than the material security of (generally) shared prosperity was the social security of being accepted as full participants in the American scheme. Why live *differently* when living the same way as everybody else made others *so nice* to us?

More importantly, though, the time of the secular-liberal-individualist order is just about up. Even if our institutions can run on fumes for a few more decades, people are increasingly fed up with a culture of alienation that benefits those with the wealth and power to exploit it, while leaving everyone else with neither material nor social (let alone spiritual) stability. The evidence is everywhere: the opioid epidemic, skyrocketing suicide rates among teens and middle-aged men, the reemergence of nationalism and socialism as explicit options in American politics, and so on. Everyone who isn't actively profiting from the current system knows that something is wrong. And as fewer and fewer people profit from the system, the tensions will only heighten.

The Church in America spent generations trying to accommodate itself to the American order. And it more or less succeeded, at least on that order's terms. (No need to rehash what I think about the effect of that success on the faithful.) But now that order, which has been in force since the Second World War and was supercharged by victory in the Cold War, is in crisis. This is not the time to double down on Americanism; it's the time to leave the table, the time finally to declare independence.

The Church should be thrilled by the growing but confused realization that liberal individualism simply doesn't work *because she has all the answers*. She can articulate *why* it doesn't work: because it doesn't accord with our nature as social beings and as creatures innately ordered to our Creator. She can articulate *how* it hasn't worked: By denying the intrinsic relationship between man and God and His Church, and by denying the necessity of solidarity, it has eroded the foundation of justice that makes a genuine society possible. And perhaps most importantly, she can articulate *and* demonstrate a new and better way: communities animated by grace and committed to the common good, which actualizes the good of each member and culminates in the eternal joy of communion with the Holy Trinity.

If we don't fill this need, others will. We're already witnessing a resurgence of identitarian ideology, which aims to build community around racial and ethnic heritage. Some will try to build social and economic utopias based on human ingenuity alone, rejecting the wisdom of the ages and the genuinely perfecting grace of Christ. Others will be drawn to communities and ideologies that offer an appealing and robust view of justice, but one which is disordered or perverted. Lastly, most will be tempted by despair—despair of the possibility of justice and communion and goodness and truth itself—leading to melancholy withdrawal at best, and spasms of nihilistic violence at worst.

As Catholics, we have a choice to make: We can continue to live as we have, more or less indistinguishable from those around us, and to continue not only to flounder as a community of faith but to do so while hitched to the sinking ship of secular liberalism. Or we can trust that grace makes something better possible, and then put it into practice.

Living Together Is Possible

We live among people everywhere—our neighbors, our coworkers, our waitresses and cashiers and baristas, and often our own family—who desperately desire real communion with other human beings, but who are paralyzed by fear of vulnerability and sacrifice and rejection. This desire is built into our very souls; it's part of our desire for eternal heavenly communion, and it's part of our social nature. As I never tire of pointing out, the first thing that our Lord says is "not good" in His creation is "for … man to be alone"[56] (Gen. 2:18, NABRE). And as St. Thomas Aquinas never tired of pointing out, there is no natural desire whose fulfillment is impossible.

And yet nearly everything about modern American civilization seems designed to frustrate this longing for communion. Popular psychology emphasizes the satisfaction of desire as the key to mental well-being, but in a relativistic and subjective way that sets everyone's desires against one another in a zero-sum battle royale. The economy is structured to reward perpetual competition over cooperation, which includes seeing commitment to interpersonal communion as being in competition with productivity. Our cities are increasingly built, both in design and affordability, for the permanently single, or at least for nothing more than temporary couplings, and certainly not for children.

I will never forget my first visit to San Francisco. My friend drove me into the city for the evening, and I've never been more taken with the natural and architectural beauty of a city. And yet something was missing. We drove past Oracle Park as fans filed in for a Giants game, and among the crowd there were hardly any children. This was a baseball game! The quintessential family entertainment! But the throng was almost all immaculate twenty-somethings, just like everywhere else in the city. Later in the drive we did come across a school with one of those "when children

---

[56] We are obliged to point out that canonically sanctioned, consecrated hermits are not only legitimate but beautiful examples of holiness. Eremitical monasticism has ancient roots in the Church, and is not about *aloneness* but *more perfect communion* with the Lord.

present" speed limit signs. And I couldn't help wondering: Are children ever present?

This flight from childbearing is perhaps the most striking and disturbing symptom of our flight from communion. Communion is, after all, essential to bearing and raising children, beginning with the bodily[57] and extending into the social — that is, actually forming and maintaining a family. It's much easier and cleaner, personally and emotionally, to avoid the whole thing. But of course what could signal civilizational despair more clearly than refusing to reproduce that civilization?

The thing is, even when we ignore and deny the reality of God and His grace, having babies is still a participation in His life-giving power. (Choosing not to have children is perhaps the purest form of atheism.) He makes that baby, and all the love he brings into the world, possible. He makes the communion between mother and child possible. He makes the little first society they form possible. His grace makes the communion essential to civilization possible.

This is the secret that faithful, joyful Catholic communities unlock. They demonstrate the real possibility of the kind of trusting intimacy with our fellow persons that, at some level, we all desire. It's not a thing of the past, nor is it possible only through some kind of drastic vow or covenant (or cultic commitment). But it does require having something in common, something that goes beyond shared convictions or a shared town or neighborhood; it requires something beyond the merely human, something that both pulls us up out of our self-obsession and allows us to be more fully who we really are. It requires a shared commitment to growing in grace.

I think people sometimes expect grace to *feel like something*, like an electric jolt coursing through the body or, at least, a distinct and

---

[57] Of course assisted reproductive technology, especially in sterile places like San Francisco, is making this less and less important.

identifiable moment of transformation. Of course many saints through the ages have been granted such visions and ecstasies, but those are few and far between. In everyday life, its presence is usually imperceptible. Even in the Eucharist, the real presence of Christ is masked by the appearance of bread and wine. Sometimes people will really *feel* the warmth of God's presence upon consuming Him — I've seen it, and been jealous of it — but most of the time He is placed on our tongue, and He tastes like a stale cracker, and we swallow, and that's that.

It took me a long time to develop even a whisper of an understanding of what grace is and how it works in our lives. I remember speaking with a theologian who said, as I have repeated here, that grace heals, elevates, and perfects our nature. And that's all well and good conceptually — it did help me on an intellectual level — but I still struggled to grasp what that *really means* in the Christian life. More than the perfect academic account of grace, it has been the experience of our community of friends that has opened my eyes, even if only in a very small way, to *what grace means* for us.

In a sentence, I'd put it like this: Grace slowly chips away at our fear of the costs of communion — with our fellow men and with God. It works on our souls quietly, filing away the calluses of vice and cynicism, making our souls more open, more receptive, more tender. It makes it feel easy and natural to say yes to a friend's request for help and, sometimes even more difficult, to a friend's offer of help. It makes it easier to forgive and forget apparent slights and it relaxes our fear of accidentally committing them. It (sometimes very slowly) breaks down our resistance to changing our routines to accommodate daily devotions such as Mass or the Rosary.

Like the proverbial boiled frog, we rarely perceive change as it occurs in the moment. But then one day we realize that habits of life, from hospitality to service to prayer, that once seemed exotic or intimidating are now *just life*. It was, in part, our own doing: We had *to choose* to accept God's invitation to grow. But the first act always belongs to grace, and soon it builds up into a spiritual superstructure that makes a more beautiful way of life possible.

The superstructure is nothing less than the Body of Christ Himself, giving a heavenly meaning and order and purpose to our lives. Grace allows us to understand and love our particular roles as members of His Body—as fathers or mothers, laborers or teachers, quiet guardians or enthusiastic evangelists or stoic leaders—both giving us confidence that we belong to something bigger than ourselves and actualizing our fullest identity in Christ.

More than just about anything else the Church can muster, robust Catholic communities show the rest of the word what it's missing. They are beacons of Catholic identity and authenticity on an increasingly featureless social landscape. And as they grow and intertwine, these communities can be the beginning of the rebirth of Catholic culture.

A New Culture

Cultural Catholicism gets a bad rap—including in this book. And for good reason: When the habits of Catholic life lose their spiritual savor, they lose what makes them truly valuable. A culture that has the trappings of Catholicism but not its substance, not its anchor in the Person and teachings of Christ, isn't just missing something: It's actively detrimental to faith, teaching other Catholics and the surrounding world that the Church has nothing genuinely special to offer, that she's merely a social club.

But that doesn't mean that Catholicism is focused only on the transcendent. That's where we always have to be pointed, of course—toward heaven, toward the angels and saints, toward the surpassing and sublime mystery of the Trinity. But, as we've said, Catholicism is also a deeply *incarnational* tradition. Beginning with the Eucharist, the Church is deeply invested in corporeality, the embodied nature of man and of the God who became man. This means that we have always had a high view of the physical, embodied traditions that make up a culture, from Christmas trees and Yule logs to meatless Fridays and raucous patronal feasts. Catholicism is always cultural; it just can't be *only* cultural.

Our vision of a network of Catholic communities promises a renewal of genuine Catholic culture. One of the most important aspects of shared traditions is that they bind people to the Church with something more than a strict assent of the mind to the truths of the Faith. As Catholic culture has dissipated into cultural Catholicism, which is in turn dissipating into nothingness, the ability of the Church to retain and attract the struggling, the doubtful, the *average* has weakened.

Now, the Church has never had too much trouble attracting those with the intelligence (and the free time) to "read themselves into the Church"—that is, to take up an independent study of St. Thomas Aquinas and St. Bernard of Clairvaux and St. John Henry Newman (himself an example of this phenomenon) and decide that Catholicism is the full truth of the universe. But that kind of intellectual experience should be only one way of coming to know Christ—and, in truth, one of the less traveled ones. A Church that attracts only exceptional converts risks becoming a Church of the elite, which she has never been and must never become. A Church of and for everyone, on the other hand, attracts and retains not just with her intellectual heritage but with the beauty of her witness, with the loving kindness of her members, and with her culture that makes it hard to desire, or even to imagine, living any other way.

One of the most striking symptoms of the collapse of a robust Catholic culture has been the collapse in the *expectation* that the next generation will keep the Faith. Today, sticking with the Church is perceived to be, and most often is, an active choice; it's no longer something that can happen passively, the way a trust fund

The Prodigal Church

kid matures into a trust fund adult, simply because *this is the way it is*. Almost all of my close friends, myself and my wife included, all roughly in our thirties, either spent significant time away from the sacraments or converted to Catholicism as adults. And even those who never wavered feel that they really had to *choose* the Church; she's no longer passed down automatically like an inheritance.

On the one hand, this voluntaristic Catholicism—based on the conscious choice of each member—has the benefit of selecting for zeal. But on the other hand, again, the Church is not truly universal—truly catholic—if she is the Church of only the zealous. She must be the Church of the everyday person: of the laborer who doesn't have the time or inclination for high theology; of the doubter who isn't so sure about the Immaculate Conception but who loves the timelessness of the Mass; of the simple woman who loves nothing more than praying her Rosary and who couldn't care less about the details of papal infallibility or the hypostatic union or whatever the "kerygma" is.

Building strong Catholic communities is, in part, about forming strong Catholics; but it's also about building a place where average or even weak Catholics can still be confidently bound to Christ and His Church, where they can thrive materially and spiritually. It's about building a whole new world, ordered toward Christ but open to everyone around us, that we might bring others to Him.

A New World

This vision of renewal through communities built on the love of friendship culminates in something more than an archipelago or even a network: a parallel society. After all, if there is no neutrality between God and secularism (*God or Nothing*, as the recent title of a book by Cardinal Robert Sarah put it), then there really is no other choice. We will either have a world of our own, built on love of God and love of neighbor, or we will be subsumed by the world of hedonism and greed and false liberty, the world of idolatry.

It has always been thus. Rapprochement between the Church and liberal secularism, while at times strategically valuable, has too often been based in the notion that secularism could remain reliably neutral between Christ and the void. But there is no neutrality, and acquiescence to the concept of neutrality always ends, in practice, with acquiescence to the void. And so, ultimately, our goal must always be conversion of the whole world to Christ, as He commanded His disciples (Matt. 28:16–20). The first step is demonstrating that a new and better world is possible.

That new and better world is nothing less than the bringing-to-life of the fullness of Catholic tradition, energized by grace and anchored in heaven, in the circumstances of the twenty-first century. It is innovation within tradition, sacrificing nothing—including the forward-thinking creativity that has always accompanied the best of Catholic renewal. We can have it all, if only we trust that, with God, everything is possible.

While the first aim in forming and maintaining community is to nurture our own friendships, in the long term, our thinking will have to expand. As more and more Catholics and converts are drawn to a more integrated, more radical way of living, the opportunities to establish real independence from the liberal, secular order will grow. It's impossible to build an enduring culture of tradition, love, and justice while relying on a culture of disordered progress, hedonism, and exploitation for meaning and sustenance. While we should prudently and cleverly put the resources of the secular order to good use,[58] we cannot remain parasitic on it forever.

---

[58] See the vexing parable of the unjust steward: "And I tell you, make friends for yourselves by means of unrighteous mammon, so that when it fails they may receive you into the eternal habitations" (Luke 16:9). We must be clear-eyed about the injustice of

The Prodigal Church

For instance, one of the most serious struggles for a growing community will be socioeconomic diversity. While initial friendships will usually be formed within roughly the same class—and there's nothing inherently wrong with this—a genuinely Catholic community must be open to all. Rising real estate prices and stagnant wages are the kinds of structural constraints, generally beyond the control of even a well-established Catholic enclave, that make full Catholic authenticity all but impossible. There are work-arounds that are truly lovely—I know of a case where a family with several children "rented out" a basement apartment to a struggling young couple in return for childcare—but for the long haul, we have to think bigger.

We have to think about creating a parallel economy, so that every Catholic can feel materially as well as spiritually and socially secure. This means starting businesses with an eye toward hiring fellow members of the community; it means establishing mutual aid and insurance societies; it means developing residential schemes that break the trend of rising prices and socioeconomic segregation, making it possible for the relatively wealthy and the relatively poor to live in proximity and solidarity. If Jews and Anabaptists can form imperfect but generally thriving parallel societies *without the benefit of the sacraments*, surely we can aim to do the same with a patient reliance on grace.

Also unlike insular religious groups, this vision of Catholic community is about transforming the world, not primarily retreating from it. It's about bringing into being a way of life that's ultimately for everyone, not just for us. But the first step toward creating

our present order, without falling into the despair or scrupulosity of complete withdrawal. The means of profit and finance can be used to build an alternative order, as long as we don't become so attached to them that we go native.

something transformative is stepping back and collecting ourselves, allowing God to repair the dissipation of the past few generations so that we can understand our own distinctiveness once again, before proposing it confidently to others.

And, yes, this long-term vision of a parallel society and economy is extravagant. It's not going to happen within a time frame satisfactory to modern attention spans, and it will ultimately be the fruit not so much of cleverness as of holiness and virtue. It's something to keep in our mind's eye, something to motivate us to build boldly, even if it doesn't come to pass in our lifetimes.

There's an old virtue, mostly passed into cultural memory now, called *longanimity*. It's the virtue of taking the long view, of regarding something beautiful on the distant horizon and striding confidently toward it. It's the virtue that motivates us to plant and to nurture a fruit tree that will not mature in our lifetime, but will feed generations to come.

This is the virtue of renewal. It is the antidote to the despair of the challenges of our age, and it flowers into a joyful hope for the future, founded in Jesus Christ.

Now Is the Time

It really is easy to get discouraged. There are the scandals, of course, that continue to trickle out of the institutional Church. There are the bickering and the politicking in Rome and in chanceries everywhere. There's disinterest among parish priests and there's dysfunction in extended families. There's all the brokenness we're confronted with every day: the stories of doubt and betrayal that are shared on social media, and the everyday difficulties in our own lives and communities.

Most of all, though, it's lukewarmness that makes renewal feel impossible. It's the wallowing in mediocrity, the apparent inability to muster even the desire to be great, to be virtuous, to be truly holy. Some of the most bracing words in Scripture were transcribed by St. John in Revelation:

> I know your works: you are neither cold nor hot. Would that you were cold or hot! So, because you are lukewarm, and neither cold nor hot, I will spew you out of my mouth. For you say, I am rich, I have prospered, and I need nothing; not knowing that you are wretched, pitiable, poor, blind, and naked.... He who has an ear, let him hear what the Spirit says to the churches. (Rev. 3:15–17, 22)

"Would that you were cold or hot!" *Do something grand! Try to be great! Take risks! If you fail, I am here for you! You are not lost!*

Yes, in many respects the Church in America has prospered over the past several decades. Scandals notwithstanding, we have achieved a level of respectability that would have been envied by every Catholic for the first two centuries of the Church's presence on these shores. But, we must always ask, at what cost? We have chosen to take on costs in faithfulness for the sake of respectability; now is the time to take on costs—any costs—for the sake of faithfulness. "Behold, now is the acceptable time; behold, now is the day of salvation" (2 Cor. 6:2).

As the Church, we are called to bring to the world not comfort and approval but a foretaste of heaven—in our prayer, in our liturgy, in the conduct of our lives, and in the organization of our families and communities. We are called to demonstrate the goodness of Christ, to bring His genuine presence into the world. We are called to demonstrate what grace makes possible. We just have to trust Him.

Out of the present crisis can come a renaissance of faith, a renewal of hope and abundant joy in the promises of Christ in this world and the next. In Him, His grace, and His Church, we have everything we need. We only have to say the word, and we shall be healed.

About the Author

Brandon McGinley has been writing about faith and politics since his regular column in his college newspaper. His career has spanned politics and publishing, from pro-life advocacy to editing EWTN books. His work has appeared in *National Review*, the *Washington Post*, *First Things*, the *Catholic Herald*, *Plough*, and the *Lamp*, among other venues. He lives in the Pittsburgh neighborhood of Brookline with his wife and four children. This is his first book.

Sophia Institute

Sophia Institute is a nonprofit institution that seeks to nurture the spiritual, moral, and cultural life of souls and to spread the Gospel of Christ in conformity with the authentic teachings of the Roman Catholic Church.

Sophia Institute Press fulfills this mission by offering translations, reprints, and new publications that afford readers a rich source of the enduring wisdom of mankind.

Sophia Institute also operates the popular online resource CatholicExchange.com. *Catholic Exchange* provides world news from a Catholic perspective as well as daily devotionals and articles that will help readers to grow in holiness and live a life consistent with the teachings of the Church.

In 2013, Sophia Institute launched Sophia Institute for Teachers to renew and rebuild Catholic culture through service to Catholic education. With the goal of nurturing the spiritual, moral, and cultural life of souls, and an abiding respect for the role and work of teachers, we strive to provide materials and programs that are at once enlightening to the mind and ennobling to the heart; faithful and complete, as well as useful and practical.

Sophia Institute gratefully recognizes the Solidarity Association for preserving and encouraging the growth of our apostolate over the course of many years. Without their generous and timely support, this book would not be in your hands.

www.SophiaInstitute.com
www.CatholicExchange.com
www.SophiaInstituteforTeachers.org

Sophia Institute Press® is a registered trademark of Sophia Institute.
Sophia Institute is a tax-exempt institution as defined by the
Internal Revenue Code, Section 501(c)(3). Tax ID 22-2548708.